MW00825003

—THE NEW—
CHARCUTERIE
COOKBOOK

—THE NEW—
CHARCUTERIE
COOKBOOK

EXCEPTIONAL CURED MEATS TO MAKE AND SERVE AT HOME

JAMIE BISSONNETTE

Chef/Owner of Toro NYC, Coppa and Toro Boston
Winner of the James Beard Best Chef: Northeast award

Photography by Ken Goodman

PAGE STREET
PUBLISHING CO.

First published in 2014 by
Page Street Publishing Co.
27 Congress Street, Suite 103
Salem, MA 01970
www.pagestreetpublishing.com

Distributed by Macmillan; sales in Canada by The Canadian Manda Group; distribution in Canada by The Jaguar Book Group.

17   16   15   14   2   3   4   5

ISBN-13: 978-1-62414-046-4
ISBN-10: 1-62414-046-7

Library of Congress Control Number: 2014934900

Cover and book design by Page Street Publishing Co.
Photography by Ken Goodman

Printed and bound in China

Page Street is proud to be a member of 1% for the Planet. Members donate one percent of their sales to one or more of the over 1,500 environmental and sustainability charities across the globe who participate in this program.

CONTENTS

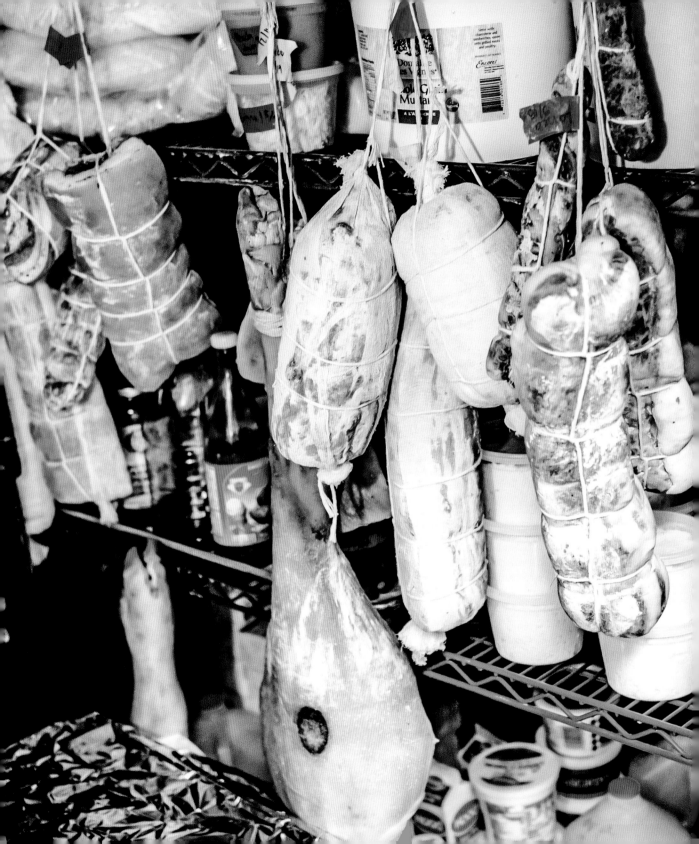

FOREWORD

I have been eating Jamie Bissonnette's food for a long time now. For years before I met him I had unknowingly been connected to him. Cooks cook. They plate. We eat. It's a pretty great relationship structure. Very one-sided. Non-committal. Perfect for most of us. Looking back in the rearview mirror I should have seen it coming. Love is like a fucking freight train when you don't see it coming, frozen on the rails like a deer in the headlights. I got greased. Bad.

Jamie is a brilliant young chef with decades of amazing work ahead of him. He's been in charge of, and associated with, some of the best restaurants in America. He has cooked with all the greats, donated his time, selflessly helped with events big and small, lent his name to food festivals from coast to coast, raised money, contributed to our lives with passion and is a devoted mentor and leader.

There are a lot of real bastards in our business but Jamie is one of the most beloved guys I know. Why should you care? What's that got to do with food? Well kids, you can't make great food; you can't put an experience in a bowl unless you have a gift for connecting with people on a deep level. There's a great Russian saying that translates loosely to "there aren't any generals in the bath house." I love that idea. When we're all naked sitting around in the steam room, there isn't a place to pin your medals. Comprende?

Jamie Bissonnette is a general in the bath house and we all know it. Here's the deal. He's obsessive, committed and superbly talented. He doesn't show off. He doesn't talk a lot . . . and never about himself unless you ask. He leads by example. He can cook his ass off. He is learned. He pays attention. He arrives early. He stays late. Shit, I love this guy.

Jamie has a curious strength, it's his strongest suit and it's ironically rare in our business. He can take ordinary food, even odd bits, fifth quarter stuff (the pluck, the viscera, the nasty to some), and make angels weep. That's real cooking. And it's why this book belongs stained and used, torn and beaten in the kitchen of every human being who owns a cutting board.

This guy will teach you about flavor, and composition and technique with only pork, salt and pepper if you want to learn how.

Let's not be ignorant, most cooking is eerily similar to the same dish down the street. Everyone has a Caesar salad on his or her menu. Kinda depressing. Jamie really cooks. 30 years ago, even in our best food cities, many of the great restaurants had chefs who were great shoppers, not necessarily soulful cooks. Hey, it happens! I like the chefs who get messy. Who really cook. Who are truly scratch. They can tell you the name of everyone who grows or raises their food. It's important. Buying great ham and slicing it thin is nice. Even I can do that. Making great ham? Another story. Different skill set. Boom.

For thousands of years everyone knew what to do with an animal. Muscles and bones, hoof to snout can be dealt with many ways. Hung to age, dried, cured, smoked or preserved. But the pluck, the organs, the blood has to be dealt with immediately, right away. To me that's the essence of great cooking. The original quick-fire challenge. The OG mystery basket of ingredients. I never liked the old quote about no one wanting to see laws or sausages get made. I think that's been our problem for generations. When you hide that stuff the quality suffers. Let's applaud it. Let's all see the sausage! Yup, I said that. Settle down, Jennings.

So the meat of the matter is that what got me punch-drunk sold on this kid was the first time I cut food with him, side-by-side, making some TV six years ago in Boston. Great, natural cook, who really understood food, and had a beautiful working methodology. Buttoned up in every way. I ate three meals at Toro then, day and night. Now Toro NYC is the hottest ticket in town.

Two years ago, Jamie cooked something for me to, as he put it, "check it out and tell me what you really think." It's the first recipe in this book and it reminds me of Vietnam every time I eat it. Jamie's cooked charcuterie is simple and approachable. His rabbit mortadella is a cult favorite in the chef world. I am thrilled to see it in this book so the gospel of rabbit and fat can be preached. A chapter to offal pleasure gives me goose bumps. To see hearts and chitterlings, and a trio of blood sausages in a contemporary, easy, simple to understand framework will advance the agenda of improving the family meal in homes all over America by leaps and bounds. Don't know how to cure meat? Neither did I until I was shown. I really hope you take the time to make every recipe in Chapter 3. Do one each week for 4 months and you will have a master's degree in curing. Chapter 4 is short—get on it. The Fried Bone recipe is way more than what it sounds like, and last June I tried it for the first time and embarrassed myself by eating so much of it that I had pork fat stains on my shirt and pants. Chapter 5 is for those that pass Chapter 3's culinary academy. It's all about flavor here. These dishes will provide a lesson plan in composing flavor in a dish that will make you a better cook even when you mix salad dressing. I can't talk about Chapter 6 because I stole all these recipes and plan on passing them off as my own next week.

Enjoy this book. Cook from it. See why cooks fall for each other real bad. And don't ever forget to look both ways at the train tracks.

Andrew Zimmern

INTRODUCTION

When I was traveling in Europe, especially France, I was blown away that so many different types of meat came out of various animals. Here, we go through so many pork loins and chicken breasts. "Where's the rest of the animal?" I always wondered.

Back home, I started making things that other chefs don't typically cook. When I worked for chef Andy Husbands at Boston's Tremont 647, I began experimenting with charcuterie during my downtime. To me, this is the essence of being a chef: buying food, fixing it up and selling it—and a big part of that is using every part of the animal.

I think you can teach anybody how to sauté a piece of trout and toast some almonds, but it takes a lot more finesse to take something like, say, blood, and make it delicious. I get satisfaction out of cooking the kinds of things that other people might not.

Gradually, I began browsing old cookbooks and meeting other chefs who shared my passion. And because chefs are huge egomaniacs, I loved getting their feedback. Now it's like we have our own support group. We trade recipes and share secrets. And sure enough, more and more odd bits are showing up on menus. Toro New York shares a building with several other restaurants. And guess what? Every single restaurant has bone marrow on the menu. People have become more adventurous.

It wasn't always this way. I definitely didn't come from a food-focused family. I started cooking very young because I loved food and my mom was a terrible cook. She'd always make some kind of chop suey. As a teenager, I became a vegetarian, and my mom said that was fine, but I'd have to cook for myself. So I did. In high school, I was in a program where they let us out of school early to get a jump-start on our "trade"—basically, whatever crappy job they thought we were qualified for. So I'd get out early and go home, make myself lunch and watch Discovery Channel cooking shows. My guidance counselor suggested a job in construction, but I knew from then on that I wanted to become a chef.

So far it's worked out OK.

A Note on Measurements & Ingredients

As you read through the book you may notice that the majority of the measurements are done in ounces instead of tablespoons, teaspoons, cups, etc. For example, a recipe may call for 2 ounces of salt rather than 4 tablespoons. The reason for this is simple: It's more accurate. As you may know, translating ingredients from one measurement to another is not a perfect science—and I've found over the years that measuring by weight (i.e., ounces) produces better results.

Tools

To measure ingredients for the recipes in this cookbook, you'll need an ounce scale, a pound scale and measuring cups. All are easily available at stores like Target or at specialty cookware shops.

Chapter One

Cooked Charcuterie

For cooks who are just starting out, charcuterie is relatively easy. These recipes are approachable, ingredients are common and easy to find, and you don't have to worry about the flavor quite so much. Plus, it's a lot more sanitary than curing. As with all of these recipes, though, don't forget to wear gloves when handling raw meat. In addition, place the metal parts for your grinder in the freezer overnight as preparation for grinding. These recipes can be stored and refrigerated in tight-fitted plastic wrap or an airtight container for about 7 days.

Many of these recipes call for casings. I buy all of my casings at sausagemaker.com.

Lemongrass and Green Curry Sausages

Yield: 16 sausages

I remember eating beetle leaf sausages on a charcoal grill street side in Ho Chi Minh City, Vietnam—talk about a transcending dining experience! Sweet and spicy grilled sausage in Pattaya, Thailand, were just as awesome. I combined them both for the Cochon 555 competition when I returned from that trip. Needless to say, I won.

4 oz (113 g) palm sugar (aka jaggery), grated

4 garlic cloves, rough chopped

1 oz (30 g) fresh ginger root, not peeled

1 red Thai (bird's eye) chili, seeds removed and minced to a paste

3 tbsp (45 g) green curry paste

Kosher salt to taste

2 oz (59 ml) fish sauce

4 oz (113 g) mint, picked

4 oz (113 g) cilantro, washed but with stems intact

4 oz (113 g) Thai basil, washed but with stems intact

4 oz (113 g) lemon grass, rough cut

10 kaffir lime leaves, fresh or frozen

4 lb (1.5 kg) pork shoulder, deboned and diced to ½-inch (1.2-cm) pieces

1 lb (450 g) pork fatback, diced

Canola oil

2 lb (900 g) Swiss chard, largest leaves possible, for wrapping sausage

Day 1

Use a mortar and pestle large enough to contain all the fresh ingredients except the Swiss chard. Mash the palm sugar to a paste. Add the garlic and ginger and continue mashing. Add the Thai chili, curry paste and fish sauce and continue mashing.

Separately, roughly chop the mint, cilantro and Thai basil. The stems from the cilantro are tasty, and the stems from the basil will add flavor and texture. Don't chop the herbs too much, as it will all be going through the grinder later.

In a large bowl, add the paste from the mortar, the chopped herbs, the lemon grass, the whole lime leaves and the diced meat. Mix to combine. Transfer to a nonreactive (glass or plastic) container and cover tightly. Refrigerate overnight.

Day 2

Set up the meat grinder, all metal parts from the freezer. Dump the mixture of meat and marinade, including any liquid in the bottom of the container, into the grinder. Grind on medium-size (¼") plate into a bowl sitting on ice. Mix the meat to combine.

Heat up a small sauté pan with a little canola oil. Pull off a ½-inch/1.2-cm piece of the meat mixture and fry in a saucepan, then taste for seasoning. Adjust with salt, fish sauce and sugar, as needed.

Rest the meat in the refrigerator for 1 hour.

(continued)

Cut the stem out of the Swiss chard.

Place meat onto the center of the Swiss chard.

Wrap it like a loose burrito.

Cook on a grill or cast-iron griddle pan.

While the sausage is chilling, cut the stem out of the Swiss chard. Cut the leaves into 4- to 5-inch (10–13-cm) squares. The cuts can be mixed, and holes are okay. Save the scraps.

To assemble the sausage, place a square of Swiss chard, shiny side down, on a flat surface. Form about 3 ounces (85 g) of the sausage meat into a rough link and place the Swiss chard in the center. Wrap like a loose burrito and place in a container with the seam side down. Repeat until all sausage meat is used. If you run out of Swiss chard, try to cobble some pieces together from the scrap. If you don't have enough, form the sausage into 3-ounce (85-g) mini burger patties, then lay some leaf scrap on the top and bottom. (These can be served like sliders).

To cook the sausages, preheat a grill or cast-iron griddle pan. Brush the grill with vegetable oil, but do not season or oil the sausages. Grill until the sausages are fully cooked. The Swiss chard will blacken and shrink, but this adds flavor.

Serve on hot dog rolls with pickles, Kimchi (page 144) and mayo, or with Nuoc Cham (page 149) and pickled oysters. Alternatively, let cool to room temperature and serve with salad.

Banana Leaf–Wrapped Porchetta

Serves 12 to 14 people

Porchetta can be prepared in many ways. Italian cooks usually start this 2-day recipe with seasoned and rolled center-cut boneless primal, or pork belly, then cook it until the center is tender and the skin is crispy, like cracklings. I love it. The skin is the best part! This recipe is for a porchetta with a tender skin and a ton of flavor. If you have any extra sausage meat, roll it in the center of this before cooking.

Porchetta

3 cups (720 g) cure (recipe below)

1 middle primal cut of pig, about 8 lb (3 kg), skin on (If you don't have a whole pig you can use pork belly, skin on.)

6 long peppers or black pepper

Butcher's twine

1 package banana leaf

The Cure

1 tsp (5 g) black pepper

1 tsp (5 g) coriander, toasted

1 tsp (5 g) fennel seed, toasted

1 tsp (5 g) fenugreek, toasted

1 stick cinnamon bark

1 oz (2 g) pink curing salt no. 1

2 cups (480 g) kosher salt

4 garlic cloves, minced

1 cup (240 g) sugar

Day 1

To prepare the cure, crush the spices in a mortar and pestle. Mix the spices with the pink curing salt, kosher salt, minced garlic and sugar.

Rub the cure on the meat side of the pork. Let cure for 24 hours in the refrigerator.

Day 2

Wipe the cure off the meat. Season with long pepper.

Place the meat skin side down on a flat surface. Roll the pork, keeping the center as tight as possible. If desired, roll the pork around any extra sausage meat.

Truss the pork like a roast, as tight as possible. To do this, cut 15 to 20 strands of butcher's twine, each 2 feet (60 cm) long. Lay them out 1 inch (2.5 cm) apart. Place the rolled porchetta on top.

Start by tying the center string. Move two strings from the center over to the left and tie another. Then move two strings over to the right and repeat. Tie every other string until you reach the end, then move back to the center and tie the remaining strings, alternating side to side.

Cut 10 additional 2-foot (60-cm) long strands of twine and lay out as before. Position the banana leaves on top of the twine in a rectangle large enough to wrap the entire porchetta. Roll the pork up in the banana leaf and retruss with twine as before.

Let the sausages rest for at least 2 and up to 12 hours in the refrigerator.

Preheat the oven to 375°F (190°C). Cook the porchetta on a wire rack on a roasting tray for 1½ to 2 hours. Rotate every 45 minutes. Cook to an internal temperature of 150°F (65°C).

Depending on your oven, you might want to cut the roast in half, but this should be done after you tie it.

Cool the sausages to room temperature. Remove banana leaves and twine, then slice thin and serve like deli meat. If you are only using a little at a time, leave the banana leaf and twine on. This porchetta can be frozen or kept in the refrigerator for 6 to 10 days.

Lebanese Lamb Sausages

Yield: 10 sausages

At Toro in Boston, we have an amazing neighbor and friend named Jay Hajj. Jay grew up in Beirut. (He's also our landlord, but I would have said nice things either way.) He is one of the most humble and natural cooks I've met. We do a few dinners a year, and he cooks all Lebanese food. He makes a version of this sausage. His is better, but he won't give me the recipe.

5 lb (2 kg) lamb shoulder, boneless, diced (½" [1.2-cm] pieces)

2 oz (57 g) kosher salt

2 cups (473 ml) red pepper purée

5 oz (142 g) pine nuts, toasted

5 garlic gloves, chopped rough

1 bunch mint, picked and chopped

2 lemons, zested and chopped

1 oz (30 g) za'atar spice

2 oz (57 g) paprika

Canola oil

Sheep casing, soaked in tepid water for 2 hours before use

Mix the meat with all other ingredients except the casing. Let the mixture marinade for a few hours or overnight, but no longer than 12 hours.

Set up the meat grinder, all metal parts from the freezer. Grind on a medium-size (¼") plate into a bowl sitting on ice. Mix until combined and sticky.

Heat up a small sauté pan with a little canola oil. Pull off a 1- to 2-inch (2.5–5-cm) piece of the meat mixture and fry in a saucepan, then taste for seasoning. Adjust as needed.

Keep the casing wet while you work with it. Slide the casing onto the funnel but don't make a knot. Put the meat in the stuffer and pack it down. Begin extruding. As the meat comes out, pull the casing back over the nozzle and tie a knot.

Extrude one full coil, about 48 inches (1.3 m) long, and tie it off. Crimp with fingers to separate sausage. Twist the casing once one way, then the other way in between each sausage. Repeat along the entire coil. Once the sausage is cased, use a sterile needle to prick any air pockets. Prick each sausage 4 or 5 times.

Repeat the casing process to use the remaining sausage.

Once the sausage is cased, place the coils on a roasting rack or towel-lined roasting pan and dry in refrigerator for 1 to 12 hours (1 hour minimum but the longer, the better).

If you have your own curing room, follow the necessary steps for your particular curing room.

When ready, cut each sausage away from the link and grill to order or poach to an internal temperature of 145°F (63°C).

Habanero and Maple Breakfast Sausages

Yield: 20 sausages

In some sausage recipes the meat is ground, then mixed. In some recipes the meat is mixed with seasoning and then ground. This one is mixed first, and here's why: Marinating the meat with the maple, spices and salt cures the meat so when it cooks it doesn't give off so much fat. This is ideal for a breakfast sausage—start off the morning with more flavor and less grease. I like to form this sausage into little patties and sauté them on the stove or cook them on the grill. If you don't want the extra work, you can bake them in cupcake tins. Seriously, it works!

3 lb (1 kg) pork butt (or any mixed, mostly lean pork scraps), diced (½″ [1.2-cm] pieces)

1½ lb (680 g) pork belly, skin off, diced

1.25 oz (35 g) kosher salt

1 bunch sage, picked and chopped fine

1 oz (30 g) habanero, roasted, peeled and seeds removed

5 garlic gloves, rough chopped

2 cups (473 ml) best-quality maple syrup

2 oz (57 g) smoked paprika

Canola oil

Mix the meat with all other ingredients. Let the mixture marinade for a few hours or overnight, but no longer than 12 hours.

Set up the meat grinder, all metal parts from the freezer. Grind on a medium- size (¼″) plate into a bowl sitting on ice. Mix until combined and sticky.

Heat up a small sauté pan with a little canola oil. Pull off a 1- to 2-inch (2.5–5-cm) piece of the meat mixture and fry in a saucepan, then taste for seasoning. Adjust as needed.

Form the sausage into patties and cook or grill. Alternatively, fill the cups of a metal cupcake pan with 2-inch (5-cm) pieces of sausage and bake at 325°F (163°C) for 15 minutes.

Goat Merguez

Yield: 12 sausages

Although goat is served all over Europe, and it's one of the most consumed meats in the world, it's generally underappreciated in the United States. But it's tasty, tender and flavorful, and it makes a wonderful sausage. Although this sausage is traditionally cased in sheep casing, for a grilled sausage plate at Toro, I prefer hank. But either would work. Serve with homemade Harissa (see page 140) and couscous for a great-tasting tapas.

4.5 lb (2.3 kg) goat meat, diced (½" [1.2-cm] pieces)

1 lb (450 g) pork belly, rind on, diced

Zest from 1 orange

1 tsp (5 g) mint, chopped

1 tsp (5 g) cumin

1 tsp (5 g) coriander

1 tsp (5 g) fennel seeds

1½ tbsp (23 g) smoked paprika

1½ tbsp (23 g) hot spicy paprika

½ tsp espelette pepper (piment d'Espelette)

1 tsp (5 g) caraway, toasted and ground

2 cloves garlic, minced

3 tbsp (45 g) nonfat dairy milk power

3 tbsp (45 g) kosher salt

½ tsp freshly ground black pepper

1½ tsp (7 g) pink curing salt no. 1

Canola oil

Sheep casing, soaked in tepid water for 2 hours before use

Set up the meat grinder, all metal parts from the freezer. Grind the meat on a small (⅛") plate into a bowl sitting on ice. Add the orange zest and the mint to the meat mixture, then cover and keep chilled while you prepare the other ingredients.

Toast the cumin, coriander and fennel seeds. Grind the spices. Blend the spices, all remaining ingredients and about ½ cup (118 ml) water for 1 minute. Pour the mixture over meat and combine.

Heat up a small sauté pan with a little canola oil. Pull off about ½ ounce (15 g) of meat and fry to taste for seasonings. Adjust seasonings if needed.

Soak the sheep casing in tepid water for 2 hours to soften before stuffing it. Keep the casing wet while you work with it. Slide the casing onto the funnel but don't make a knot. Put the meat in the stuffer and pack it down. Begin extruding. As the meat comes out, pull the casing back over the nozzle and tie a knot.

Extrude one full coil, about 48 inches (1.3 m) long, and tie it off. Crimp with fingers to separate sausage. Twist the casing once one way, then the other way in between each link. Repeat along the entire coil. Once the sausage is cased, use a sterile needle to prick any air pockets. Prick each sausage 4 or 5 times.

Repeat the casing process to use remaining sausage.

Once the sausage is cased, place the coils on a roasting rack or towel-lined roasting pan and dry in refrigerator for 1 to 12 hours. (Let the sausage dry for at least 1 hour but the longer, the better).

If you have your own curing room, follow the necessary steps for your particular curing room.

When the sausage is ready, cut each sausage away from the link and grill to order or poach to an internal temperature of 145°F (63°C).

(continued)

Keep the casing wet while you work with it.

Begin extruding the meat.

Extrude one full coil about 48 inches (1.3 m) long, and tie it off.

Prick a hole in the sausage so air escapes and they don't explode while cooking.

Crimp with your fingers to separate the sausage. Twist the casing once one way . . .

Then the other way in between each link. Repeat along the entire coil.

Chipotle Turkey Meatloaf

Feeds 4 to 6 people

Turkey is awesome. So many people only like it around holidays like Thanksgiving. It's tragic. Great turkey has so much flavor, and making a meatloaf with turkey is a great way to showcase it. Plus, it's healthy! I've had some great wild turkey tacos in Mexico and took the idea of those flavors for this recipe. Think of it like spicy Thanksgiving leftovers.

1 cup (240 g) Spanish onion, peeled and diced

1 tbsp (15 g) garlic, chopped

2 tbsp (30 g) butter

3 tbsp (45 ml) Worcestershire sauce

⅓ cup (79 ml) chicken stock

2 tsp (10 ml) chipotle pepper purée (from a can with adobo)

1 lb (450 g) ground turkey

¾ cup (180 g) bread crumbs

2 eggs

½ cup (118 ml) ketchup

2 tbsp (30 g) parsley, picked and chopped

1 tsp (5 g) kosher salt

1 tsp (5 g) black pepper

1 tsp (5 g) cinnamon

Canola oil

Preheat oven to 325°F (163°C).

In a medium-size (¼") pan sweat the onions and garlic in butter until they are tender and clear. Add the Worcestershire sauce, chicken stock and chipotle paste, then mix to combine. Cool to room temperature.

Combine the ground turkey, bread crumbs, eggs, ketchup, onion mix and parsley in a large bowl. Mix to combine completely. Season with salt, pepper and cinnamon.

Heat up a small sauté pan with a little canola oil. Pull off a 1- to 2-inch (2.5–5-cm) piece of the turkey mixture and fry in a saucepan, then taste for seasoning. Adjust as needed. Shape into a rectangular loaf or pack into a greased terrine mold.

Bake for 1½ hours or until the internal temperature reaches 160°F (71°C). Serve hot or chill and serve cold as a sandwich. Remember, if you want to serve it cold, season more aggressively because flavors dull as they cool.

The Importance of Simply Done Turkey Breast

Yield: 4 pounds (1.5 kg) of turkey

As a kid growing up, I always loved turkey sandwiches and turkey quesadillas—they're my guilty pleasure. I always wanted a turkey sandwich on my menu, but every time I made it, the roast turkey was very dry. I experimented a lot with brine to get the breast to stay moist. Once you've carved this and you get to the ends, cook them up with cream of mushroom soup and sour cream and make an awesome "Shit on a Shingle."

4 lb (1.5 kg) boneless turkey breast, skin on

Salt

Black pepper

For the Sachet

1 tbsp (15 g) coriander

1 tbsp (15 g) fennel seed

1 tbsp (15 g) black pepper

1 tbsp (15 g) whole star anise

½ tsp caraway

2 or 3 sprigs rosemary, chopped with stems intact

20 cloves garlic, chopped rough

3 white onions, diced large

4 fresh bay leaves

1 sprig thyme

For the Brine

1 gal (3.8 l) water

¾ cup (180 g) kosher salt

¾ cup (180 g) sugar

For the Sachet

Assemble all items for sachet, wrap in cheese cloth and tie tightly.

For the Brine

Combine sachet, water, salt and sugar in large pot. Heat on low to dissolve salt and sugar. Cool before using. (To cool faster, use ¾ gallon [2.8 l] water and ¼ gallon [0.95 l] ice.) Discard sachet.

Once the brine is cool, put it in turkey breast. Let it sit in the refrigerator for 4 days. Every day pick up the turkey breast and squeeze it like a sponge. After day 4, pat it dry then dry it in the refrigerator for 4 hours.

Preheat oven to 325°F (163°C). Season the turkey breast with salt and pepper. Roast it in oven, skin side up, about 45 minutes, rotate breast, and roast an additional 30 minutes, or until internal temperature reaches 155°F (68°C).

Serve the turkey breast hot or let it cool and slice it like deli meat. For storing, cut the breast into thirds, then wrap each third tightly in plastic wrap for storage.

Country Pâté for My Dad

Yield: 2 pâtés, serving 10 to 12 people

I've looked at lots and lots of pâté recipes over the years, and many of them are complicated. When I asked my dad, who's more of a novice cook, which recipe he prefers, he said "The one you taught me." This is that recipe. It's really fresh and bright. And if you use a really good cognac, which I recommend, you'll get a lusciously nutty, caramelized flavor.

1 lb (450 g) pork belly, diced (½" [1.2 cm]) and kept chilled

½ lb (227 g) pork shoulder or duck meat, diced small and kept chilled

½ lb (227 g) duck livers, diced small and kept chilled

1½ cup (360 g) bread crumbs, any kind you have on hand or panko

3 large eggs

½ tsp pink curing salt no. 1

Kosher salt (to taste)

½ tsp espelette pepper (piment d'Espelette)

½ tsp mace, ground

Pinch paprika

1 tsp (5 g) freshly ground black pepper

2 garlic cloves, crushed

¼ cup (59 ml) cognac, Armagnac, or brandy

½ cup (120 g) chopped dried prunes

½ cup (120 g) toasted chopped pistachios

Canola oil

10 slices bacon

Set up the meat grinder, all metal parts from the freezer. Grind the meat on a small (⅛") plate sitting in a bowl on ice. Mix the meat to combine.

Add in all ingredients except the bacon. Mix to combine.

Heat up a small sauté pan with a little canola oil. Pull off a 1-inch (2.5-cm) piece of the pâté, fry and taste for seasoning. Adjust with more salt if needed.

Preheat the oven to 350°F (176°C). Line a terrine mold with the bacon so it hangs over both sides about 1½ inch (3.7 cm). Fill the mold with the pâté. Bang the terrine mold on a table to remove any air. Fold the bacon over the top, and press down to make it flat and compact. Cover the terrine.

Boil 6 to 8 cups (1.4 l to 1.9 l) water. In a deep casserole pan large enough to hold the terrine mold, pour in hot water. Put the mold in. The water should come up 2 inches (5 cm) on the side of the terrine mold.

Cook for 45 minutes, rotate the pan, and cook for 35 minutes more. Use a thermometer to check the core temperature in the middle of the pâté. It is done at 155°F (68°C). Then remove the pan from the oven, place it on a towel (or other safe surface) and cool to room temperature.

Press with pâté into the terrine mold with 2 to 5 pounds (900 g–2 kg) of pressure for 2 hours or overnight. Keep the pâté in the refrigerator for at least 3 days and up to 1 week to ripen. Remove and serve with your favorite crackers.

(continued)

Pack the terrine mold a little at a time for even layering.

Pat the pate down a little bit at a time to eliminate any air pockets.

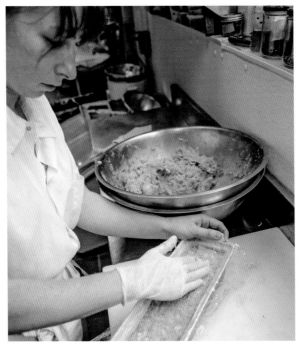

Once the mold is filled, press down on the pate to make it flat and compact.

The Best Slab Bacon

Feeds 15 to 20 people (In other words, this is a lot of bacon!)

Most people take bacon for granted, but once you've tasted homemade bacon you may never go back to Oscar Mayer. Homemade bacon is much more interesting in part because of the cure. The palm sugar I use here gives this bacon depth of flavor, but you could substitute an equal amount of maple sugar candy for a different taste.

4–6 lb (1.8–2.7 kg) slab pork belly with skin on

For the Cure

4 cups (960 g) salt

2 cups (480 g) palm sugar

4 tbsp (60 g) pink curing salt no. 1

4–5 tbsp (60–75 ml) crushed black pepper

1 tsp (5 g) chili flakes

4 tsp (20 g) yellow mustard seed

15 cloves garlic

Smoking chips

Trim the pork belly up square. Place the pork belly on a large baking sheet. Rub and massage the cure into both sides. Place on a rack over a tray, cover tightly and place in the refrigerator for 5 days.

The meat will give off a lot of liquid, so the rack and tray are important. Check the meat every day to make sure enough cure is touching the pork belly. Flip it over every day and baste with liquid. After 5 days push on the middle of the pork; if it feels firm, it's done. If not, let it cure 1 or 2 more days, checking for firmness each day.

Once the meat is done curing, rinse the belly and pat dry. Set the chips on fire using one pan, then smother out with a small amount of water. Transfer the smoldering chips to the bottom half of a two-part perforated/nonperforated pan. Put the pork belly in the top, then cover tightly with tin foil. Poke 1 or 2 small holes in tin foil for smoke to escape. Cold smoke for 1 hour.

Cook the belly in a 200°F (93°C) oven until it reaches an internal temperature of 155°F (68°C). Let cool completely, then remove the skin.

Before serving, cut ½-inch (1.2 cm) thick slices and cook in a cast-iron pan until crisp on the outside and gooey on the inside.

To make bacon croutons, cut off a piece of bacon. Mix 3 parts water to 1 part sugar with a teaspoon or two of fish sauce, then poach the bacon. When done, fry the poached bacon in a cast-iron pan. Note: The bacon can be frozen indefinitely.

(continued)

Trim the pork belly up square.

Place the pork belly on a large baking sheet, then rub and massage the cure into both sides.

Check the meat every day to make sure enough cure is touching the pork belly.

Pork Roll, a New Jersey Classic

Yield: 10 packages of pork rolls

If you know anyone who grew up in New Jersey, chances are they know Pork Roll. Developed in the 1800s by John Taylor, it was originally called Taylor Ham, and some folks still call it that. Like scrapple, I had to try it—and I loved it. I searched through many a cookbook and online for a recipe, to no avail—so working backward from the ingredients list on a package, I played around to develop this recipe. It tastes a bit like Canadian bacon.

1 lb (450 g) pork fatback, diced medium (1" [2.5-cm] pieces)

Beef middles for casing

3 lb (1 kg) pork shoulder, diced small (½" [1.2-cm] pieces)

7 oz (200 g) pork skin

½ cup (120 g) sugar

2 tbsp (30 g) kosher salt

2 tsp (10 g) garlic powder

2 tsp (10 g) ground nutmeg

2 tsp (10 g) ground white pepper

1 tsp (5 g) mace

1 oz (2 g) pink curing salt no. 1

3 tsp (15 g) whole black pepper, toasted

½ cup (118 ml) white wine

Canola oil

Place diced fatback in cold water, then bring to simmer on stove. Simmer 1 hour. Strain and cool. Discard liquid.

Soak beef middles in water for 1 hour before using.

Set up the meat grinder, all metal parts from the freezer. Grind the pork shoulder, fat and skin using the medium-size (¼") plate into a bowl sitting on ice.

Mix all the dry ingredients with the white wine to make a paste.

In an electric standing mixer with a paddle, combine all ingredients and paddle for 6 minutes on medium setting.

Heat up a small sauté pan with a little canola oil. Pull off a 1- to 2-inch (2.5–5-cm) piece and fry in a saucepan, then taste for seasoning. Adjust with salt and sugar as needed.

Keep beef casing wet while you work with it. Slide the casing onto the funnel but don't make a knot. Put the meat mixture in the stuffer and pack it down. Begin extruding. As the meat comes out, pull the casing back over the nozzle and tie a knot.

Extrude one full coil, about 32 inches (0.9 m) long, and tie it off. Crimp with fingers to separate sausage into 8-inch (20-cm) lengths. Twist the casing once one way, then the other way in between each sausage link. Repeat along the entire coil. Once the meat is cased, use a sterile needle to prick any air pockets. Prick each sausage 4 or 5 times.

Alternatively, wrap the meat in plastic wrap to make sausages about 7 to 8 inches (18–20 cm) long and 4 to 6 inches (10–15 cm) in diameter. To seal, tie the ends tightly with butcher's twine; then tie the center twice with twine so the wrap doesn't explode.

Set up a large steamer on the stovetop. Steam the sausages until they reach an internal temperature of 165°F (74°C). Cool completely, then slice by hand or on a deli slicer.

Serve these sausages pan fried on a bulkie roll with a slice of cheese and either scrambled eggs or a fried egg.

Red Curry Pâté

YIELD: 2 PÂTÉS

I've been making and sampling pâté for over 15 years, and most recipes use the same ingredients over and over in different ratios. When I started cooking at home with curry and playing with Southeast Asian ingredients, I wanted to incorporate them into my recipes, but it wasn't until I tried curry paste that I could produce the right flavor consistently. This one tastes a lot like a traditional European pâté with a hint of tanginess.

2 lb, 4 oz (1.1 kg) pork shoulder, diced to ½" x ½" (1.3 x 1.3 cm) pieces

6 lb (2 kg) pork belly, diced to ½" x ½" (1.3 x 1.3 cm) pieces

5 oz (142 g) pork kidney, diced to ½" x ½" (1.3 x 1.3 cm) pieces

3 lb (1 kg) pork liver, diced to ½" x ½" (1.3 x 1.3 cm) pieces

3 tsp (15 g) pink curing salt no. 1

3 tsp (15 g) quatre épices

½ tsp (2 g) nutmeg

5 oz (142 g) kosher salt

1 oz (30 g) minced raw garlic

1 oz (30 g) espelette chili flakes

5 oz (142 g) red curry paste

10 eggs

10 oz (300 g) bread crumbs

1¼ cups (285 ml) cognac, brandy or bourbon

Canola oil

Set up the meat grinder, all metal parts from the freezer. Grind the pork shoulder, pork belly and pork kidney on a small (⅛") plate into a bowl sitting on ice.

Grind the liver on a large (½" [1.3 cm]) plate. Mix all the meat to combine.

Mix all the dry ingredients and distribute evenly over the top of the meat. Mix to combine, then add eggs, bread crumbs and cognac and mix to combine.

Heat up a small sauté pan with a little canola oil. Pull off a 1-inch (2.5-cm) piece of the pâté, fry and taste for seasoning. Adjust with more salt if needed.

Preheat the oven to 325°F (163°C). Rub the inside of the terrine mold with canola oil. Fill the mold with the pâté. Bang the terrine mold on a table to remove any air. Put the top on the terrine.

Boil 6 to 8 cups (1.4 l to 1.9 l) water. In a deep casserole pan large enough to hold the terrine mold, pour in hot water. Put the mold in. The water should come up 2 inches (5 cm) on the side of the terrine mold.

Bake for 60 minutes to an internal temperature of 150°F (65°C). Then remove from the oven and set the terrine mold on a towel (or other safe surface) to cool to room temperature.

Rabbit Mortadella

Feeds 10 people

I've always loved bologna and mortadella. Once, as a young chef, another chef and I both ordered rabbit. We ended up with too much, so I started experimenting with diced rabbit. I tried it once in a recipe for pork mortadella but it didn't work—the end result was very dry. I tweaked the recipe by adding less pork fat and more sugar to bind it and ended up with this standby recipe. As for the taste of rabbit? Think richer chicken.

10 oz (285 g) pork fat

1 lb (450 g) boneless rabbit, diced

½ cup (120 g) pork fat, kept separate

2 tbsp (30 ml) white beer or dry white wine

¼ oz (7 g) granulated or powdered garlic

¾ oz (21 g) kosher salt

1 tsp (5 g) sugar

½ tsp pink curing salt no. 1

10-12 oz (284–340 g) crushed ice, left in freezer

½ tsp fresh grated nutmeg

1 tsp (5 g) espelette chili flakes (piments d'Espelette)

2 tsp (10 g) ground black pepper

½ cup (120 g) toasted pistachios

1 tbsp (15 g) whole black pepper corns

1 large beef middle (casing, soaked in water for 1 hour, or use plastic wrap)

Butcher's twine

Dice ½ cup (70 g) of pork fat, then blanch for 2 minutes in water. Let cool completely while you grind the rabbit meat.

Combine rabbit with beer or wine, garlic, salt, sugar and pink curing salt.

Set up the grinder with the small (⅛") plate. For the first round, grind the rabbit mixture. Next, grind 10 oz (285 g) pork fat on top of the rabbit. Mix with ⅓ of ice and grind again. Add another ⅓ of ice and grind again. Add the last ⅓ of ice as well as all spices (except for whole black peppercorns) and pepper and grind again. (You will grind a total of 3 times with ice).

Mix the blanched pork fat with toasted pistachios and whole black peppercorns. Fold the fat, nuts and peppercorns into the rabbit mixture. Pull off a 1-inch (2.5-cm) piece, wrap it tightly in plastic wrap and poach. Taste and adjust seasonings.

Keep the beef casing wet while you work with it. Slide the casing onto the funnel but don't make a knot. Put the rabbit mixture in the stuffer and pack it down. Begin extruding. As the meat comes out, pull the casing back over the nozzle and tie a knot.

Extrude one full coil, about 48 inches (1.3 m) long, and tie it off. Crimp with fingers to separate sausage. Twist the casing once one way, then the other way in between each sausage link. Repeat along the entire coil. Once the rabbit is cased, use a sterile needle to prick any air pockets. Prick each sausage 4 or 5 times. Repeat the casing process to use remaining rabbit.

Alternatively, wrap rabbit meat in plastic wrap to make sausages about 7 to 8 inches (18-20 cm) long and 3 to 4 inches (7.6-10 cm) in diameter. Tie ends tightly to seal with butcher's twine, then tie the center twice with twine so the wrap doesn't explode.

Bring a large pot of water to simmer, then turn off the heat. Drop in the sausages, cover with a towel, and poach for 15 minutes or until internal temperature reaches 150°F (65°C). Chill in an ice bath.

You can store this rabbit in the refrigerator for up to 2 weeks. To serve, slice like bologna. Serve thick slices with mustard or grill like fried bologna.

Foie Gras Sausage

Yield: 20 sausages

One of the first sausages I learned to make was Boudin Blanc, a white sausage typically made with pork. This is a more luxe version of that dish—essentially a creamy, emulsified sausage with great flavor and texture.

2½ lb (2.5 kg) pork butt, diced to ½" x ½" (1.3 x 1.3 cm) pieces

1 lb (450 g) fatback, diced to ½" x ½" (1.3 x 1.3 cm) pieces

1 lb (450 g) foie gras scrap

½ lb (225 g) crushed ice

Ginger powder to taste

Nutmeg to taste

1¼ oz (35 g) kosher salt

Cayenne to taste

2 eggs

1 cup (237 ml) heavy cream

2 tsp (10 g) curing salt no. 2

½ oz (14 g) dextrose

2½ oz (70 g) milk powder

Canola oil

Hank casing, soaked in tepid water for 2 hours before use

To make the casing, set up the meat grinder, all metal parts from the freezer. Grind pork butt, fatback and foie gras on the small (⅛") plate into a bowl sitting on ice. Add ½ cup (118 ml) of the ice and grind again.

Combine ginger, nutmeg, kosher salt and cayenne in a small bowl. Use a paddle to incorporate the spice mix with the meat. Add the eggs one at a time, then add the heavy cream slowly. Add the curing salt no. 2, dextrose and milk powder.

Heat up a small sauté pan with a little canola oil. Pull off a 1-inch (2.5-cm) piece of the meat, fry and taste for seasoning. Adjust seasonings as needed.

Keep the casing wet while you work with it. Slide the casing onto the funnel but don't make a knot. Put the meat in the stuffer and pack it down. Begin extruding. As the meat comes out, pull the casing back over the nozzle and tie a knot.

Extrude one full coil, about 48 inches (1.3 m) long, and tie it off. Crimp with fingers to separate sausage. Twist the casing once one way, then the other way in between the sausage links. Repeat along the entire coil. Once the sausage is cased, use a sterile needle to prick any air pockets. Prick each sausage 4 or 5 times.

Repeat the casing process to use remaining sausage.

Once the sausage is cased, place the coils on a roasting rack or towel-lined roasting pan and allow to dry in the refrigerator for 1 to 12 hours (1 hour minimum but the longer, the better).

If you have your own curing room, follow the necessary steps for your particular curing room.

When ready, cut each sausage away from the link and grill to order or poach to an internal temperature of 150°F (65°C).

Bologna with Vietnamese Flavors

Yield: 4 one-pound (450 g) pieces (This is a lot, but they can be frozen after cooking.)

I love the Vietnamese sandwiches, banh mi. My favorite one is with traditional cold cuts, liver spread, boiled ham, headcheese, pâté and bologna. I've seen the bologna for sale in Vietnam and in markets in Boston but I couldn't find a recipe. I also wanted to make one with heritage pork, so I started using a mortadella recipe and tweaking it with what I knew from the bologna label: fish sauce, palm sugar and wrapped in banana or lotus leaf. Eight years later and I've settled on this recipe. This recipe is traditionally called a 3:2:1 farce, meaning approximately 3 parts meat, 1 part fat, 1 part ice. Although the proportions I use here don't match that equation exactly it will still produce a great-tasting dish. It's an old-school, emulsified sausage recipe.

3 lb (1 kg) pork shoulder, deboned and diced to ½" x ½" (1.3 x 1.3 cm) pieces

1 lb, 2 oz (500 g) pork fatback, diced to ½" x ½" (1.3 x 1.3 cm) pieces

10 oz (300 g) ice cubes

4 oz (113 g) palm sugar, grated

1 oz (30 g) kosher salt

¾ oz (10 g) garlic powder

½ oz (14 g) whole black pepper corns, toasted

1 oz (2 g) pink curing salt no. 1

1 red Thai bird chili, seeds removed and minced to a paste

⅞ cup (200 ml) fish sauce

Canola oil

1 package banana leaves

Plastic wrap

Put the diced meat in the freezer for 1 to 2 hours. Break up ice and store that in the freezer as well.

Set up the grinder with the small (⅛") plate. For the first round, grind the meat and the fat together into a metal bowl resting on ice. Add ⅓ of the ice from the freezer and do it again. Repeat this process until you have used all the ice, adding the sugar in with the meat on the last grind. The meat should look like pink paste.

In a small bowl combine the salt, garlic powder, peppercorns, cure salt, Thai chili and fish sauce. Stir to combine. Add the salt mix to the meat and knead like dough until the mixture is sticky and all ingredients are thoroughly mixed in.

Heat up a small sauté pan with a little canola oil. Pull off a 1-inch (2.5-cm) piece of the meat, fry and taste for seasoning. Adjust seasonings as needed.

Chill the meat in the refrigerator until ready to use.

When the meat is ready, cut the banana leaf into 10-inch by 30-inch (26 x 78 cm) rectangles. Place ⅓ of the farce toward the front of the leaf. Roll the farce in the leaf so the leaf overlaps a bit. Wrap it again in plastic wrap, then tie tightly with twine at both ends and three times throughout the length of the sausage. This is a messy process. It will seep out the sides and make a mess. Just keep cleaning as you go, and save the excess for restuffing.

In a pot large enough to hold the sausages plus double the volume of water, bring the water to boil. Place the sausages in the water, turn the heat off and cover with a dishcloth. Set a timer for 15 minutes. The sausage is done when the internal temperature reaches 160°F (71°C).

Remove the sausage, shock in an ice bath and store in the refrigerator. When the sausage is ready, remove the plastic wrap and banana leaf. Slice or dice as desired.

Rabbit and Beer Pâté

Yield: 2 Pâtés

I first saw this pâté made in Europe by a German chef, and, given its delicious flavor, I assumed it had lots and lots of ingredients. But it turns out the beer provides (even dictates!) the flavor of the terrine, eliminating the need for many other ingredients. I prefer witbier (Dutch for "white beer"). For a fruitier and funkier version of this 2-day recipe (as well as gluten free), substitute Basque (Spanish) cider for the beer.

2 lb (900 g) boneless rabbit meat, diced to ½" x ½" (1.3 x 1.3 cm) pieces

4 oz (113 g) rabbit kidney (or mix of rabbit organ meats), diced to ½" x ½" (1.3 x 1.3 cm) pieces

1 lb (450 g) pork belly, diced to ½" x ½" (1.3 x 1.3 cm) pieces

3 fresh bay leaves

2 sprigs thyme

1 tsp (5 g) chopped tarragon

1 tsp (3 g) pink salt

1¼ cup (298 ml) beer

Salt to taste

Pepper to taste

20 slices Serrano ham

Canola oil

Day 1

Mix all meat together with bay leaves, thyme sprigs, tarragon, salt and beer. Cover and marinate overnight.

Day 2

Remove the bay leaves and sprigs of thyme; set aside leaves and sprigs for later use.

Set up the meat grinder, all metal parts from the freezer. Grind the meat on a small (⅛") plate into a bowl sitting on ice. Season with salt and pepper

Heat up a small sauté pan with a little canola oil. Pull off a 1-inch (2.5-cm) piece of the pâté, fry and taste for seasoning. Adjust with more salt if needed.

Preheat the oven to 325°F (163°C). Place the bay leaves and sprigs of thyme in the bottom of the mold. Line the mold with ham, leaving enough ham hanging over the edges to cover the pâté. Fill the mold with the pâté. Bang the terrine mold on a table to remove any air. Fold the ham over to cover the pâté. Put the cover on the terrine.

Boil 6 to 8 cups (1.4 l to 1.9 l) water. In a deep casserole pan large enough to hold the terrine mold, pour in hot water. Put the mold in. The water should come up 2 inches (5 cm) on the side of the terrine mold.

Bake for 60 minutes to an internal temperature of 160°F (71°C). Then remove from the oven and put the terrine mold on a towel (or other safe surface) to cool to room temperature.

Spanish Chorizo

Yield: Five 8-ounce (225 g) sausages

I've always loved making paella, and I thought it would be really great to make my own cured sausage to use in my paella. While this cured chorizo works great for that it can also be served on its own. I like it best paired with Monchego cheese.

1.875 lb (0.85 kg) pork shoulder, diced to ½" x ½" (1.3 x 1.3 cm) pieces

0.3 oz (8 g) Insta cure #2

0.4 oz (11 g) kosher salt

0.35 oz (10 g) tequila, brandy or sherry

4 cascabel chilis, seeds removed and chopped

5 garlic cloves, crushed

0.625 lb (0.3 kg) fatback, diced to ½" x ½" (1.3 x 1.3 cm) pieces

0.03 oz (2 g) light brown sugar

1 tbsp (15 g) sweet smoked paprika De la Verra

2 tsp (10 g) spicy smoked paprika De la Verra

1 tsp (4 g) esplette

Canola oil

Sheep casing or hank, soaked in tepid water for 2 hours before use

Mix pork shoulder, salts, liquor, chilis, and garlic in large bowl, then refrigerate for 24 hours. Cut the fatback into small cubes. Mix with brown sugar and seasonings.

Set up the meat grinder, all metal parts from the freezer. Grind the pork shoulder, then the fatback, on a large (½" [1.3 cm]) plate into a bowl sitting on ice. Mix the ground meats to combine.

Heat up a small sauté pan with a little canola oil. Pull off a 1- to 2-inch (1.3–2.5-cm) piece and fry in a saucepan, then taste for seasoning. Adjust seasonings as needed.

Keep the sheep casing wet while you work with it. Slide the casing onto the funnel but don't make a knot. Put the meat in the stuffer and pack it down. Begin extruding. As the meat comes out, pull the casing back over the nozzle and tie a knot.

Extrude one full coil, about 48 inches (1.3 m) long, and tie it off. Crimp with fingers to separate sausage. Twist the casing once one way, then the other way in between sausage links. Repeat along the entire coil. Once the sausage is cased, use a sterile needle to prick any air pockets. Prick each sausage 4 or 5 times.

Repeat the casing process to use remaining sausage.

Once the sausage is cased, place the coils on a roasting rack or towel-lined roasting pan and dry in 70°F (21°C) for 12 hours. Then move to cool airy, dark room to ripen for 5-6 weeks.

If you have your own curing room, follow the necessary steps for your particular curing room. Grill the sausage to order or poach for about 12 minutes to an internal temperature of 145°F (63°C). Cool, then cut in half and grill both sides until hot.

Mexican Chorizo

Yield: 20 sausages

When most people think of chorizo, they think of a smoky, dried sausage from Spain or Portugal. Mexican chorizo, however, is a crumbly sausage made with vinegar. While traveling in Mexico, somewhere between Playa del Carmen and Tulum, I stopped at a roadside market and learned this recipe.

5 lb (2 kg) pork butt, diced to ½" x ½" (1.3 x 1.3 cm) pieces

2.2 lb (1 kg) pork belly, diced to ½" x ½" (1.3 x 1.3 cm) pieces

0.4 oz (10 g) cumin

0.2 oz (6 g) fennel

0.4 oz (10 g) coriander

1 cup (237 ml) tepid water

2 cloves garlic, chopped rough

6½ tbsp (100 g) powdered dextrose

0.6 oz (16 g) curing salt no. 2

3.2 oz (90 g) nonfat dairy milk powder

3.8 oz (107 g) kosher salt

2.2 oz (62 g) Hungarian paprika

4.4 oz (134 g) smoked paprika de La Vera

1 tbsp plus 1 tsp (20 ml) cider vinegar

0.3 oz (8 g) cascabel chili powder

0.5 oz (15 g) black pepper, freshly ground

Canola oil

Sheep casing, soaked in tepid water for 2 hours before use

Set up the meat grinder, all metal parts from the freezer. Grind on the medium-size (¼") plate into a bowl sitting on ice. Mix the meat to combine.

Toast the cumin, fennel and coriander, then grind. Mix the remaining ingredients with the water and purée in blender.

Heat up a small sauté pan with a little canola oil. Pull off a 1- to 2-inch (2.5–5-cm) piece and fry in a saucepan, then taste for seasoning. Adjust seasonings as needed.

Keep the sheep casing wet while you work with it. Slide the casing onto the funnel but don't make a knot. Put the meat in the stuffer and pack it down. Begin extruding. As the meat comes out, pull the casing back over the nozzle and tie a knot.

Extrude one full coil, about 48 inches (1.3 m) long, and tie it off. Crimp with fingers to separate sausage. Twist the casing once one way, then the other way in between sausage links. Repeat along the entire coil. Once the sausage is cased, use a sterile needle to prick any air pockets. Prick each sausage 4 or 5 times.

Repeat the casing process to use remaining sausage.

Once the sausage is cased, place the coils on a roasting rack or towel-lined roasting pan and dry in the refrigerator for 12 hours.

If you have your own curing room, follow the necessary steps for your particular curing room.

Grill the sausage to order or poach for about 12 minutes to an internal temperature of 145°F (63°C). Cool, then cut in half and grill both sides until hot.

Chapter two

Offal-y Good Charcuterie

My strength is making offal delicious—looking at ingredients and treating them with thoughtfulness. Taking parts and tongues and getting flavor into them is more interesting to me than, say, just opening up an avocado. Just remember: In this case, freshness is important. Things rot. Your recipes are only as good as the quality of the ingredients. All of these recipes keep for up to 7 days in the refrigerator unless indicated otherwise.

Lobster and Sweetbread Terrine

Yield: 1 mold, feeds roughly 12 people

I've always loved the classic French combination of lobster and sweetbreads (ris de veau). I wanted to create this same flavor in a cold appetizer that could be passed around. While a lot of pâtés are rustic, the addition of sweetbreads in this 2-day recipe gives it a little more elegance.

3 cups (910 ml) whole milk

½ lb (240 g) sweetbreads

½ lb (450 g) caul fat

½ lb (240 g) pork or chicken livers, diced to ½" x ½" (1.3 x 1.3 cm) pieces

1 onion, diced small

Butter

1 lb (450 g) pork belly, diced to ½" x ½" (1.3 x 1.3 cm) pieces

½ lb (240 g) pork shoulder, diced to ½" x ½" (1.3 x 1.3 cm) pieces

3 cloves garlic, minced

2 tsp (10 g) chopped tarragon

⅛ oz (4 g) nutmeg

0.07 oz (2 g) ground cinnamon

¼ oz (7 g) espelette chili flakes

2 g curing salt no. 1

3 eggs

7 oz (198 g) bread crumbs

1 cup (237 ml) apple jack whiskey

¼ cup (60 g) toasted chopped hazelnuts

½ lb (240 g) cooked lobster, diced to ½" x ½" (1.3 x 1.3 cm) pieces

Soak sweetbreads in milk overnight. Soak caul fat in water overnight.

The next day, poach sweetbreads in salted, simmering water for 3 minutes, then cool to room temperature. Peel the skin off and use your hands to break into ½" x ½" (1.3 x 1.3 cm) chunks.

Cook onion in butter until tender, then set aside.

Set up the meat grinder, all metal parts from the freezer. Grind pork belly, shoulder and livers on the small (⅛") plate into a bowl sitting on ice. Mix the meat to combine.

Add in all ingredients except lobster, sweetbreads and caul fat. Mix to combine. Preheat the oven to 350°F (176°C).

Fold in lobster and sweetbreads. Line a terrine mold with caul fat, leaving enough hanging over the sides to cover the top without overlapping. Fill the mold with the pâté. Bang the terrine mold on a table to remove any air. Fold the caul fat over the top and press down to make it flat and compact. Put the cover on the terrine.

Boil 6 to 8 cups (1.4 l to 1.9 l) water. In a deep casserole pan large enough to hold the terrine mold, pour in hot water. Put the mold in. The water should come up 2 inches (5 cm) on the side of the terrine mold.

Cook for 45 minutes, rotate the pan, and cook for 35 minutes more. Use a thermometer to check the core temperature in the middle of the pâté. It is done at 155°F (68°C). Then remove it from the oven, and cool the terrine mold on a towel (or other safe surface) to cool to room temperature.

Rabbit and Pork Liverwurst

Yield: 1 pound (450 g)

When I was a little boy, I would sit in the grocery cart while my mother shopped. To keep me occupied, she gave me one of my favorite snacks: a kosher pickle with a slice of liverwurst on it. Later, when I was a young chef, I noticed how chefs cooking with rabbit typically throw away the rabbit livers. I experimented with the rabbit livers, adapting a recipe I had for liverwurst, and made this recipe for the first time when I was 21 years old.

½ lb (227 g) pork liver, diced to ½" x ½" (1.3 x 1.3 cm) pieces

¾ lb (342 g) pork belly, diced to ½" x ½" (1.3 x 1.3 cm) pieces

1 onion, diced medium

2 cups (473 ml) water

1 cup (237 ml) dry white wine

½ lb (227 g) rabbit liver, diced to ½" x ½" (1.3 x 1.3 cm) pieces

2 tsp (10 g) salt

½ tsp fresh black pepper

½ tsp nutmeg

¼ tsp ground clove

¼ tsp espelette chili flake

¼ tsp urfa pepper

Simmer diced pork liver, pork belly and onion in water and wine for 75 minutes. Drain, reserving liquid.

Simmer diced rabbit liver in reserved water. Turn off heat and let poach slowly for 5 minutes. Drain mixture, reserving liquid.

Set up the meat grinder, all metal parts from the freezer. Grind all meats on small (⅛") plate into a bowl sitting on ice. Repeat grind 3 or 4 times.

Strain ⅔ cup (160 ml) of reserved liquid through cheesecloth. Add spices and mix with the ground meat until completely emulsified. Pack into jars, ramekins or terrine mold and chill overnight.

Easiest Chicken Liver Mousse

Yield: One 1-pound (450 g) mousse, feeds about 15 people

One of the first things a young chef learns to make is Chicken Liver Mousse. I learned it but didn't make it often enough to remember the recipe. One day I watched a sous chef make it in less than 10 minutes, including the time for soaking the livers. I was so impressed that I set a goal to do the same—and the result is a recipe I turn to over and over again. It's buttery, creamy and tart.

1 lb (450 g) chicken livers

3 cups (710 ml) whole milk

Salt to taste

Pepper to taste

¼ tsp cayenne pepper

Vegetable oil

½ lb (450 g) unsalted butter

3 shallots, rough cut

1 tbsp (15 g) butter

3 cloves garlic, rough cut

2 sprigs thyme

2 fresh bay leaves

¼ cup (59 ml) cognac or brandy

1 tbsp (15 g) esplette

Schmaltz (rendered chicken fat; page 151) for storage

Soak the chicken livers overnight in milk, then strain them. Place the livers on a clean towel to dry.

Season the chicken livers with salt, pepper and cayenne. Panfry in vegetable oil on stovetop, checking both sides until medium rare. Place the warm, cooked livers in a food processor with unsalted butter.

Add butter to the pan and cook shallots and garlic. Add thyme and bay leaf. Scrape the bottom of pan to get the fond. When the shallots are tender, add cognac (or brandy). Remove bay leaf and thyme.

Pour into food processor with esplette. Blend until combined. Season with salt and pepper. Pour directly into a dish or ramekin, cover the top layer with schmaltz (rendered chicken fat) and store in the refrigerator. For a very creamy version of mousse, strain the mixture through a fine-mesh sieve using paddle, then pack it into jar or mold.

(continued)

Remove the livers from milk, and mat dry before seasoning.

Pan sear the liver over moderate heat, cooking to medium rare.

Deglaze the pan with bourbon, cognac or any favorite brown spirit.

Purée the mixture while still warm.

Season the livers with salt.

Add the room temperature butter a little at a time.

Season with esplette.

Plate the liver mousse.

Chitterling and Tripe Sausages

Yield: 15 sausages

I read about this recipe, which is a traditional sausage from Normandy, for years. While I was traveling in Paris with my dad, I made him order it, knowing it would be funky. Neither of us liked the chewy texture or musty flavor. Years later, working off memory, I experimented and developed this recipe. Turns out there are two tricks to eliminating the chewy texture and the musty flavor: Cook the tripe longer, and cook the chitterlings until they're tender.

½ lb (227 g) honeycomb tripe

4 cups (0.95 l) white wine

2 cups (473 ml) white wine

1 cup (227 g) salt

1 gal (3.8 l) chicken stock

Small sachet with 1 tsp (5 g) each: caraway, coriander, fennel seed and mustard seed

½ lb (227 g) pork chitterlings

4 cups (945 ml) white wine

1 tbsp (15 g) butter

3 garlic cloves, minced

2 white onions, julienned

½ lb (227 g) pork fatback

2 tsp (10 g) quatre épices

¼ tsp (1 g) ground nutmeg

½ tsp (2 g) cayenne

Salt and pepper to taste

1 cup (237 ml) Normandy cider

1 tsp (5 g) Dijon mustard

Lard or duck fat

If the tripe is frozen, defrost it in cold water in refrigerator. Soak it in water with 4 cups (0.95 l) white wine for 3 to 12 hours.

Discard the water and white wine and clean the tripe by scrubbing it with the blunt side of a French knife. Rinse, then put it in a pot of cold water with 2 cups (473 ml) white wine and 1 cup (237 g) salt and cover the pot.

Bring to simmer. Turn it off immediately and strain. Return the tripe to a pot and cover with 4 inches (10 cm) chicken stock. Add sachet. Bring to boil, reduce to low simmer, cover with tight-fitting lid and cook for 5 to 6 hours.

Cool the tripe overnight in its liquid (if possible, cool in a metal container set in ice so it will be easier to heat again). Once the tripe is cool, strain the cooking liquid and set it aside. Julienne tripe.

Soak chitterlings overnight in white wine. Blanch the chitterlings in tripe liquid for 15 minutes.

Combine butter, garlic, onion and fatback and cook down over low heat, without letting it brown, until onions are tender and fat is rendered.

Add quatre épices, nutmeg, cayenne and chitterlings and cook 5 to 10 minutes over medium heat. Stir frequently and don't let brown. Add julienned tripe, season with salt and pepper. Add cider and mustard. Cook alcohol out, about 3 minutes. Season and let cool.

Hand-stuff sausages using a funnel and the back of a spoon. Push stuffing into the funnel with casing wrapped around funnel. Squeeze by hand to make tight sausages. Tie off 6-inch (15-cm) links and prick air holes all over. Hang or dry in refrigerator or curing room for 10 to 15 hours.

To cook the sausages, gently panfry in lard or duck fat over low to medium heat (to prevent bursting). They should be hot all the way through, with a temperature of 160°F (71°C). Serve with sautéed onions and apple calvados (brandy) or sautéed cabbage and a side of whole-grain mustard.

Whipped Pork Butter with Truffle and Honey

YIELD: 4 CUPS (920 G)

When you butcher a whole animal, there's a great deal of fat left over, but some of it is too soft for use in making sausage. I was intrigued by whipping lard to make pork butter, so I developed this recipe. Whipped pork butter has the consistency of butter but tastes like whatever you flavor it with, since fat and alcohol absorb flavor easily.

5 lb (2 kg) pork fat (any type, including skin, etc.), rough cut into small chunks

4 shallots, rough cut

4 cloves garlic, rough cut

2 fresh bay leaves

2 or 3 sprigs thyme

1 sprig rosemary

2 cups (473 ml) water

1 cup (235 ml) dry white wine

7 oz (200 g) black truffle peelings or fresh black truffle (depending on season)

Fleur de sel

Kosher salt

¼ cup (59 ml) honey

Place fat, shallots, garlic, bay leaves, thyme, rosemary, water and wine into a heavy-bottom pot with a lid. Cook on low heat to render. Cook for 3 hours, just below simmer, adding water if needed to prevent burning. Stir every 15 to 20 minutes.

Once the fat is rendered, pass it through a fine-mesh sieve. Cool it in an ice bath until solid. Once it's cool, place it in a mixer that has a cookie paddle. Add black truffles and both types of salt and whip until airy.

Store this butter in an airtight containers or jars. (It can be frozen indefinitely.) Serve on toast and drizzle with honey.

Beef Heart Pastrami

Yield: 1 heart

I work with a lot of local farmers, and they always have hearts and tongues left over after butchering. I experimented with a number of variations until I arrived at this garlicky recipe, which we use on everything from pizza to crostini at Toro.

1 fresh or frozen beef heart, 3 to 5 lb (1 to 2 kg)

For the Cure

2 cups (480 g) kosher salt

1 cup (240 g) sugar

2 tbsp (30 g) coriander

2 tbsp (30 g) whole black peppercorns

2 tsp (10 g) chili flakes

2 tbsp (30 g) fennel seed

1 tsp (5 g) caraway

For the Pastrami Spice Mix

¼ cup (60 g) smoked paprika

3 tbsp (45 g) coriander

2 tbsp (30 g) yellow mustard seed

¼ tsp caraway

1 tbsp (15 g) white peppercorns

2 tbsp (30 g) black peppercorns

3 tbsp (45 g) brown sugar

8 cloves garlic, minced

Salt to taste

Pepper to taste

If using frozen beef heart, allow to thaw in fridge. Using jacquard, punch 10 holes on each inside and outside of the beef heart. Rub it vigorously with cure mix, then cure it in the refrigerator for 36 hours. If the heart dries out, dust it with additional cure mix.

Grind all pastrami spices (except brown sugar and garlic) on coarse grind. Mix in brown sugar and garlic.

Brush the cure off the beef heart, then season it with salt and pepper. Rub the beef heart with pastrami spice mix; apply generously.

Preheat oven to 350°F (176°C). Roast the beef heart about 30 minutes or to an internal temperature of 140°F (61°C). (The beef heart can also be grilled.)

Cool and refrigerate. Slice thin, like deli-style roast beef.

Smoked Beef Tongue

Yield: 1 tongue

I remember going to delis when I was growing up and seeing huge smoked tongues hanging behind the counter. When I tried it, I loved it, so I taught myself how to make it, then perfected the recipe so it's tender and delicious. Many people don't like tongue because of the texture, but cooking it like this solves that problem.

1 fresh beef tongue, about 3 lb (1 kg)

For the Cure

2 cups (480 g) kosher salt

1 cup (240 g) sugar

2 tbsp (30 g) coriander

2 tbsp (30 g) whole black peppercorns

2 tsp (10 g) chili flakes

2 tbsp (30 g) fennel seed

1 tsp (5 g) caraway

Smoking chips

2 cups (473 ml) mirepoix

Use the jacquard to punch the whole tongue evenly about 20 times. Rub the tongue in the cure mix and refrigerate it for 48 hours.

Set the chips on fire using one pan, then smother the fire with a small amount of water. Transfer the smoldering chips to the bottom half of a two-part perforated/nonperforated pan. Put the tongue in the top, then cover it tightly with tin foil. Poke 1 or 2 small holes in tin foil for smoke to escape. Cold smoke for 1 hour.

Place the tongue in a stockpot and cover with 1 inch (2.5 cm) of water. Add mirepoix. Bring to a boil, then turn down to just above simmer and cook 2 hours.

Remove the tongue and cool it in an ice bath. When it's cool enough to handle, peel off the outer skin. Wrap the tongue in plastic wrap and store in the refrigerator.

When ready to serve the tongue, slice it thin like deli meat for sandwiches or cut thick slices and grill. This also works nicely warmed up with chicken stock and served with lentils.

Blood Sausage for Beginners

Yield: 20 sausages

Making blood sausage is a daunting task. Many cooks avoid it, but I never did. Maybe it's my love for the band Slayer's "Reign in Blood" album or the fact that I loved shocking people with foods as a young cook, but I learned and taught myself how to make many kinds of blood sausages. Of all the recipes out there, this one is the easiest. They have a spinach-y flavor, with hints of iron.

3 lb (1 kg) pork butt (or any mixed, primarily lean pork scraps), diced to ½" by ½" (1.3 x 1.3 cm) pieces

1½ lb (675 g) pork belly, skin off, diced to ½" x ½" (1.3 x 1.3 cm) pieces

1¼ oz (35 g) kosher salt

3 garlic cloves

1 tbsp (15 g) espelette pepper (piment d' Espelette)

1 tsp (5 g) chili flakes

0.75 oz (21 g) fresh black pepper

3 cups (710 ml) pig's blood—the fresher, the better (if you have to use frozen pig's blood, spin it in a blender after it's thawed)

1 cup (128 g) nonfat dairy milk powder

4 tbsp (67.5 g) powdered dextrose

2 tbsp (15 g) quatre épices, 4-spice, or terrine spice

0.07 oz (2 g) curing salt no. 1

Canola oil

Hog casing, soaked in tepid water for 2 hours before use

Set up the meat grinder, all metal parts from the freezer. Grind on a medium-size (½" [1.3 cm]) plate into a bowl sitting on ice. Mix the meat to combine.

In a mortar and pestle, mash the salt and garlic into a paste. Add the piment d'Espelette, chili flakes and black pepper. Combine the garlic mix with the pig's blood and whisk to incorporate. Add the milk powder, dextrose, 4-spice and curing salt no. 1. Pour the blood mixture over the ground meat and mix thoroughly until the meat is sticky.

Heat up a small sauté pan with a little canola oil. Pull off a 1- to 2-inch (2.5–5-cm) piece and fry in a saucepan, then taste for seasoning. Adjust with salt, pepper or whatever spice needs tweaking.

Case the sausages, then tie them into 2- to 3-inch (5–7.6-cm) links. Hang overnight to set. If you do not have room to hang them in the refrigerator, tie them off and set them on a rack in front of a clean fan. (If there's dust on the blades, then the sausage will be dirty.)

In a pot large enough to hold the sausage plus double the volume of water, bring the water to boil. Place the sausages in the water, turn the heat off and cover with a dishcloth. Set a timer for 15 minutes. Check the temperature of the sausage. Remove the sausage when it reaches an internal temperature of 155°F (68°C). Cool on a tray with cloth.

From here, the sausage can be eaten, stored and reheated or served cold.

To reheat it, I like the sausage baked in a very hot oven, pan fried or grilled.

Buttifara Negra (Blood Sausage for Intermediate Cooks)

Yield: 15 sausages

I've had a hard time teaching my cooks how to make blood sausage, so I came up with this recipe to create another "rung" on the ladder in terms of learning. If you're experienced with sausage making, then this recipe is a fine starting point, but if you're truly a beginner, I recommend the Blood Sausage for Beginners recipe on page 64.

2 cups (473 ml) pig's blood

1 lb (450 g) chicken livers

1 tsp (5 g) espelette chili flakes

1 tsp (5 g) pink salt

½ tsp quatre épices

2 cups (473 ml) heavy cream

1 egg

Hank or hog casing, soaked in tepid water for 2 hours before use

Blend all ingredients in a blender.

Keep the casing wet while you work with it. Slide the casing onto the funnel but don't make a knot. Put the mixture in the stuffer and pack it down. Begin extruding. As the mixture comes out, pull the casing back over the nozzle and tie a knot.

Extrude one full coil, about 48 inches (1.3 m) long, and tie it off. Crimp with fingers to separate the sausages. Twist the casing once one way, then the other way between each sausage link. Repeat along the entire coil. Once the sausage is cased, use a sterile needle to prick any air pockets. Prick each sausage 4 or 5 times. Repeat the casing process to use remaining sausage.

Cook the sausage on stovetop 20 to 30 minutes or to an internal temperature of 170°F (76°C). Cool to room temperature. The sausage can be sliced and served as cold tapas or grilled.

Smoked Tongue Bocadillo

Serves 1

A lot of people are afraid of the flavor of sea urchin—but its salty and sour taste blends perfectly with the smoky flavor of the beef tongue. I refer to this as a funkier version of pastrami with Russian dressing.

1 tsp (5 g) Dijon mustard

1 tsp (5 g) mustard

4-5 slices Smoked Tongue (see recipe, page 62)

4 oz (110 g) piece Ciabatta bread, cut in half

3-4 pieces sea urchin, each one about ½" (1.3 cm) in length

Mix the two mustards together and spread on one side of the bread. Layer with tongue and sea urchin. Butter second piece of bread and place face down on sea urchin.

Butter two remaining sides of bread and grill on stovetop or in Panini pan.

Boudin Noir (Blood Sausage for Ninjas)

Yield: 15 sausages

This recipe isn't hard for accomplished cooks, but the reason I call it Blood Sausage for Ninjas is because there is so much room for error. You need to pay attention to every step along the way, pay attention to the details, when making this recipe. This has a bloodier flavor—and it picks up a lot of onion flavors as well, making it sweet and custardy.

3 lb (1 kg) fatback, skin off, diced

2 fresh bay leaves

2 sprigs thyme

3 lb (1 kg) Spanish onions, diced small

1 garlic clove, minced

1 tbsp (15 ml) cognac or apple jack

2 cups plus 2 tbsp (500 ml) heavy cream

1 tsp (5 g) brown sugar

2 qt (2 l) pig's blood

½ cup (118 ml) whole milk

½ tsp mace, ground

3 tbsp (45 g) kosher salt

½ cup (118 g) bread crumbs, finely ground

Sheep's casing or hog hank, soaked in tepid water for 2 hours before use

Render the fatback with the bay leaves and the thyme. Strain the liquid, saving the rendered fat and the diced fat.

Place the rendered fat in a large pot and sweat the onions and garlic until very tender. Add the cognac and cook off the alcohol. Add the reserved diced fat. Add the heavy cream and sugar and scald.

While the cream scalds, whisk the blood and milk together with the spices, salt and breadcrumbs.

Temper the blood (milk mixture with the onion mixture).

Keep the casing wet while you work with it. Slide the casing onto the funnel but don't make a knot. Put the mixture in the stuffer and pack it down. Begin extruding. As the mixture comes out, pull the casing back over the nozzle and tie a knot.

Extrude one full coil, about 48 inches (1.3 m) long, and tie it off. Crimp with fingers to separate sausages. Twist the casing once one way, then the other way between each sausage link. Repeat along the entire coil. Once the sausage is cased, use a sterile needle to prick any air pockets. Prick each sausage 4 or 5 times. Repeat the casing process to use remaining sausage.

Bring a large pot of water to boil. As it boils, add the sausage (don't crowd, the water should stay at a constant 180°F [82°C]). Cook until the juice in the sausage runs clear when pricked or until the internal temperature is 155°F (68°C).

Cool the sausages on a tray. I like these sausages peeled, then fried with eggs, butter and apples.

Cockscombs

Yield: 3 quarts (2.8 L), feeds up to 20 people

The first time I saw these in a European market I couldn't believe people ate them. I tried them and found they didn't taste like much but the texture was really cool. I sampled other recipes and found the same thing—they didn't have much flavor, but the texture was great. Cockscombs are very porous, so I tried cooking them with assertive flavors to give them depth.

1 lb (450 g) cockscombs

¼ cup (60 g) Schmaltz (page 151)

1 white onion, diced small

4 cloves garlic, minced

1 fresh bay leaf

Salt to taste

Pepper to taste

3 tbsp (45 g) smoked paprika

3 tbsp (45 g) spicy paprika

2 cups (473 ml) Basque cider

1 qt (0.95 l) chicken stock

1 carrot, diced medium

3 tbsp (45 ml) red wine or sherry vinegar

Soak cockscombs in water overnight. Pull them from the water and pat dry. Trim about 1 inch (2.5 cm) or so off bottom of the combs (where they attach to the skull).

Put schmaltz, onion, garlic and bay leaf in a sauté pan. Cook over low heat until translucent and tender (but not caramelized). Season cockscombs with salt and pepper, then add them to the schmaltz mixture, stirring to coat. Add both types of paprika, then add cider. Reduce cider, add chicken stock and bring to simmer. Cover tightly and cook in a 250°F (121°C) oven for 1 hour.

Add carrot, then lower the oven temperature to 200°F (93°C) and cook for another hour. To check doneness, pinch the cockscombs with your fingers or a pair of tweezers. The combs should be tender all the way through. If not, put them back in the oven for 30-minute intervals, using more chicken stock as needed. Adjust seasonings, then add red wine or sherry vinegar.

Serve the cockscombs warmed up over rice or sauté mushrooms and serve cockscombs with mushrooms and a poached egg. They can also be frozen indefinitely.

HEADCHEESE

YIELD: 2 TERRINE MOLDS

One of the first recipes you hear about as a young chef is headcheese, and what I heard was that it's bad and people don't like it. Naturally, I wanted to make it so people would love it! It took some work, but I finally came up with a method for tenderizing, moistening and flavoring this rich meat.

1 pig's head, 8–11 lb (3–4 kg)

2 lb (900 g) mirepoix, wrapped in cheesecloth

1 small sachet containing 1 tsp (5 g) each: black peppercorn, coriander, fennel seeds, mustard seeds, garlic, tarragon, thyme and juniper

1 bottle of white wine

Fresh herbs

Espelette or black pepper

Salt to taste

Favorite vinegar

FOR THE BRINE

4 gallons (15 l) water

2 cups (480 g) salt

¼ cup (60 g) sugar

Small sachet containing 2 tsp (10 g) black peppercorn, 10 garlic cloves, 4 tsp (20 g) fennel seeds and 2 tsp (10 g) coriander seeds

To make the brine, warm water to 100°F (37.7°C), dissolve salt and sugar, add sachet and cool.

Cover the pig's head with cold water and let it sit at room temperature for 8 hours or put it in the walk-in refrigerator overnight. Put the pig's head into the brine and let it sit for 3 days. Then strain off the liquid and discard.

Place the pig's head into a pot large enough to cover with water that is 6 inches (15 cm) higher than the head. Add mirepoix, sachet and wine to pot.

Bring to a boil and skim, then lower to a simmer and let cook, uncovered, for 6 to 8 hours. Strain, saving the liquid and the head. Discard the sachet and mirepoix.

Reduce the poaching liquid rapidly, skimming and clarifying as needed.

When the head is cool enough to handle but still warm, pick the meat from the skull. Squeeze the fat into small pieces, and pull the flesh into strips. Place the meat, fat, and flesh strips into a bowl, and season with fresh herbs, espelette or black pepper, salt and vinegar.

Add ½ cup (118 ml) of the reduced poaching liquid, then mix with a spoon until it resembles a soft cheese spread.

Pour the mixture into a terrine mold or loaf pan, and let it set up overnight. Let it ripen from 2 to 30 days.

Serve this headcheese with mustards and salts.

(continued)

To make the brine, warm the water, dissolve the salt and sugar, and add the sachet.

Place the pig's head into a pot large enough to cover with 6 inches (15 cm) of water.

Remove the head from the pot.

Strain the pot, saving the liquid.

The meat should pull from the bone without tearing.

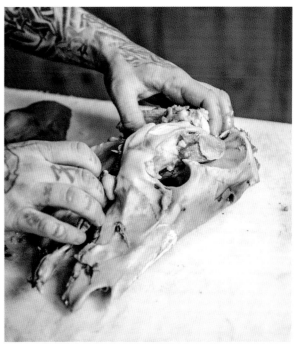

When the head is cool enough to handle but still warm, pick the meat from the skull.

The skull, picked clean.

Chapter three

Hide the Salami

These are cured items. They do not get cooked—which sounds easy, but it's actually very tricky and takes lots of patience. It's like making bread, or beer, or wine: It takes time and energy. But for me, it's also the most rewarding. When I brewed my first beer, I had to wait for it to turn into something. When it was finally ready, I thought, "Man, this is kind of awesome. I just made something that I had to let nature ferment for me." Curing gives me the same feeling. Unless indicated otherwise, these dishes can be refrigerated, uncovered, for a couple of months.

Simply Perfect Duck Prosciutto

Yield: 2 breasts

I love charcuterie, and over the years people have asked me for nonpork versions of prosciutto. Marc Orfaly, former chef at Pigalle, taught me this recipe, and I fell in love with the flavors. At Coppa, we use ducks from Bella Bella Gourmet Foods, and the breasts are so thick they cure beautifully without a lot of spice.

6 cups (1.4 kg) salt

3 cups (720 g) sugar

3 tbsp (45 g) coriander

1 cinnamon stick, crushed

2 tbsp (30 g) fennel seed

3 tbsp (45 g) yellow mustard seed

3 tbsp (45 g) whole black peppercorn

2 fresh bay leaves

3 sprigs thyme

2 (8-oz [227-g]) duck breasts

2 bunches cheesecloth, 18″ (45 cm) long

3 ft (0.9 m) butcher's twine

Mix salt, sugar and all dry spices. Dry off duck breasts. In a mixing bowl, cover duck breasts with salt mixture and massage gently.

Fill the bottom of a large nonreactive (glass or plastic) pan with 1½″ (3.7 cm) salt mixture. Put the duck breasts in the pan, skin side down, and cover with remaining salt mixture. Wrap with plastic wrap and refrigerate for 36 hours.

Remove the duck breasts from the pan and brush off salt with a damp cloth. Discard salt.

Wrap the breasts in cheesecloth and tie tightly with twine. Age 10 to 15 days in the refrigerator or in a curing room. Slice thin to serve. They can keep in the refrigerator for up to six months. Wrap them tightly, and change the wrap as needed.

COPPA

YIELD: 1 (3 ½-POUND [1.6-KG]) COPPA

I knew I was going to name my restaurant Coppa well before I knew I was opening one. The first time I had a slice of coppa, the dude called it gabbagoul. It was salty, spicy, fatty and wicked tasty. When I learned to make it, I fell in love. Plus, butchering the muscle out of the neck and shoulder is one of my favorite things to cut.

5 lb (2 kg) pork neck (ask a butcher to harvest this cut)

FOR THE CURE

½ cup (120 g) kosher salt

2 tbsp (30 g) espelette chili flakes

½ tbsp (7 g) black pepper

1½ tbsp (25 g) powdered dextrose

1 tsp (5 g) curing salt no. 2

Cheesecloth

Combine salt, espelette, black pepper and dextrose with curing salt no. 2, then divide the mixture in two.

Using one half of the mixture, rub the meat all over. Place the meat in a nonreactive (glass or plastic) container and refrigerate for 7 days. Check on the meat every day, rubbing with a bit more cure mix.

After 7 days, rinse the coppa. Rub with the remaining cure, then wrap in cheesecloth.

Incubate the meat for 12 hours at room temperature (70°F–80°F [21°C–26°C]). Hang it in a curing room at 60°F–70°F (15°C–21°C) for 190 to 200 days or until it's firm.

Slice thin and serve chilled or slice thick and grill to order. This can be refrigerated, wrapped, for up to 6 months.

(continued)

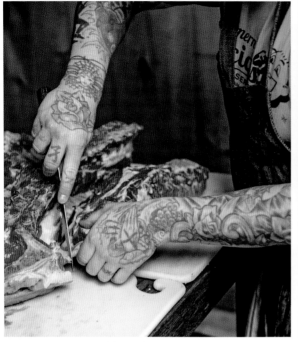

Cutting the coppa out of the neck.

The raw coppa.

Use one half of the mixture and rub the meat all over.

Check on the meat every day, rubbing with a bit more cure mix.

Rosso di Pepe

Yield: 1 (6 pound [2.7 kg]) ham

Rosso means "red" and di pepe means "peppery." So that should tell you what this recipe produces: a beautiful red ham with peppery, floral flavors.

8 lb (3.6 kg) boneless pork shoulder, skin on

For the Cure

12 cups (2.8 kg) kosher salt

¼ oz (9 g) curing salt no. 1

6 cups (1.4 kg) sugar

2 tbsp (30 g) minced garlic

3 tbsp (45 g) whole coriander

1 tbsp (15 g) whole juniper berry

1 tbsp (15 g) whole black peppercorns

1 cup (237 g) black pepper

½ cup (118 ml) dry red wine

Butcher's twine

Cheesecloth

Trim the pork shoulder to a rectangular shape.

Mix all salts, sugar and spices together to make the cure. Divide the mixture into 2 portions. Place the pork shoulder skin side up. Rub ½ of the cure all over the skin; massage heavily; flip it over and massage the cure into the meat, especially crevices. Cover with plastic wrap and cure in the refrigerator for 8 days, skin side down.

Check the shoulder every day. If it looks dry, sprinkle with additional cure. After 8 days, flip it over and heavily cure the skin side (¼-inch [6-mm] thick layer of cure all over). Rewrap and cure for 4 additional days.

On day 4 place the shoulder on a dry towel. Use a firm brush or second clean towel to brush off all the cure. Combine the black pepper and red wine in a blender to make paste. Place the shoulder skin side down. Rub the paste all over the inside of the pork shoulder.

Fold the shoulder together, then roll it as tight as possible. Truss with twine—make 5 ties, 1 in the middle and 2 on each side. Wrap in 2 layers of cheesecloth and truss again with 5 ties. Tie the rolled pork very tight on both ends.

Hang in a dedicated refrigerator or curing room for 200 days. Watch for mold or moisture. If the cheesecloth gets wet, remove it and replace it with fresh cheesecloth.

At 200 days if the shoulder feels firm throughout, then it's done. If not, cure it for an additional 30 days. When it is ready to serve, cut off the skin and slice it like deli meat. This ham can be refrigerated, wrapped, for up to 6 months.

(continued)

Position the ham or other cured meat on the slicer.

Position your hand below the slicer as the meat comes off.

Catch the sliced ham in your hand.

Alternatively, gently pull the sliced meat away from the slicer. Slice the ham as thin as possible without tearing.

Saucisson Sec, the Classic

Yield: 7 sausages

Walking around Paris, you can see tiny sausages hanging everywhere, and I really wanted to make them at home. This is a simple, traditional French sausage—and the challenge in developing this recipe was balancing just a few ingredients with quality meat to make a tangy, delicious sausage.

4½ lb (2 kg) pork meat

½ lb (225 g) fatback

1½ oz (40 g) kosher salt

¼ to ½ oz (10 g) black pepper, coarsely ground

½ oz (15 g) dextrose

¼ oz (6 g) curing salt no. 2

⅔ oz (18 g) garlic, minced to a paste

¼ cup (59 ml) dry white wine

Sheep or hog casing, soaked in tepid water for 2 hours before use

Set up the meat grinder, all metal parts from the freezer. Grind the pork meat and fatback on a large (¾" [1.9 cm]) plate into a bowl sitting on ice. Use a paddle to mix in all other ingredients.

Keep the casing while you work with it. Slide the casing onto the funnel but don't make a knot. Put the mixture in the stuffer and pack it down. Begin extruding. As the mixture comes out, pull the casing back over the nozzle and tie a knot.

Extrude one full coil, about 48 inches (1.3 m) long, and tie it off. Crimp with fingers to separate sausages into 12-inch (30-cm) lengths. Twist the casing once one way, then the other between each sausage link. Repeat along the entire coil. Once the sausage is cased, use a sterile needle to prick any air pockets. Prick each sausage 4 or 5 times. Repeat the casing process to use remaining sausage.

Hang the sausages to cure 18 to 20 days at 60°F–75°F (18°C–21°C). These can be refrigerated, wrapped, for up to 6 months.

Saucisson Sec with Indian Flavors

Yield: 7 sausages

I'd been making the same sausage for a while, but at the same time I'd been experimenting with yellow curry in vinaigrettes. I made one batch of sausage with curry, and it was so different I knew I was on to something. I played around and eventually came up with this 2-day recipe.

2 tbsp (30 g) black peppercorns

White wine for soaking peppercorns

3½ lb (1.6 kg) pork shoulder, diced

1½ lb (680 g) fatback, diced

4 tsp (20 g) curry powder

2 tsp (10 g) espelette chili flakes

2 cloves garlic, minced

¼ cup (57 g) kosher salt

1 tsp (5 g) curing salt no. 2

3 tbsp (45 ml) dry white wine

Hog casing, soaked in tepid water for 2 hours before use

Day 1

Cover black peppercorns generously with white wine and soak overnight.

Set up the meat grinder, all metal parts from the freezer. Grind pork and fatback on a small (¼") plate into a bowl sitting on ice. Combine curry, espelette, peppercorns, garlic, salt and curing salt no. 2. Mix with a fork until combined.

Set up a standing mixer with a paddle. Add meat, wine and salt mixture. Paddle for 3 minutes until it looks sticky. Cover tightly with plastic wrap and let it rest in the refrigerator overnight.

Day 2

Keep the casing wet while you work with it. Slide the casing onto the funnel but don't make a knot. Put the mixture in the stuffer and pack it down. Begin extruding. As the mixture comes out, pull the casing back over the nozzle and tie a knot.

Extrude one full coil, about 48 inches (1.3 m) long, and tie it off. Crimp with fingers to separate sausages into 8-inch (20-cm) lengths. Twist the casing once one way, then the other way between each sausage link. Repeat along the entire coil. Once the sausage is cased, use a sterile needle to prick any air pockets. Prick each sausage 4 or 5 times. Repeat the casing process to use remaining sausage.

Hang the meat, refrigerated, for 30 to 40 days, or until the sausage loses about ⅓ of its weight. It's done when it feels firm all over.

Serve these sausages sliced with pickles and mustard. They can be refrigerated, wrapped, for up to 6 months.

Lomo di Cerdo

Yield: 1 (3 ½-pound [1.6-kg]) lomo

This recipe is the same as the one for Coppa (page 79), but we're using a center-cut pork loin instead of a shoulder. These two cuts of meat have different muscle structure: The loin doesn't have as much intermuscular fat, meaning it's a leaner cut. Because there's less moisture to dry out, it takes about 30 days less curing time than the coppa. Be sure to buy the freshest center-cut pork loin you can—I recommend avoiding those in the supermarket bins. Instead, seek out a fresh cut from the butcher.

4 oz (113 g) kosher salt

2 tbsp (30 g) espelette chili flakes

2 tsp (10 g) black pepper

1½ tbsp (25 g) powdered dextrose

0.2 oz (6g) curing salt no. 2

5 lb (2 kg) very fresh center-cut pork loin, diameter of 3–4″ (7.6–10 cm)

Cheesecloth

Combine salt, espelette, black pepper and dextrose with curing salt no. 2, then divide the mixture in two.

Using one half of the mixture, rub the meat all over. Place the meat in a nonreactive (glass or plastic) container and refrigerate for 7 days. Check on the meat every day, rubbing with a bit more cure mix.

After 7 days, rinse the meat. Rub it with the remaining cure, then wrap in cheesecloth.

Incubate for 12 hours at room temperature (70°F–80°F [21°C–26°C]). Hang it in a curing room at 60°F–70°F (15°C–21°C) for 160 to 170 days or until firm.

Slice the lomo thin and serve chilled, or slice thick and grill to order. It can be refrigerated, wrapped, for up to 6 months.

Arctic Char Gravlax

Yield: 2 ½ pounds (1.2 kg) of gravlax

One of the first things I learned in culinary school was how to cure salmon. The truth is, that I hated it. I found most recipes used farm-raised salmon, which doesn't have much flavor to start with, or overcured it to make the fish too salty. I wanted to improve it, starting with really good quality salmon. In Iceland, the arctic char I had was buttery and clean, and I knew this was the place to start. I added the liquor and voilà!—an easy recipe that tastes great.

8½ oz (300 g) muscovado sugar

5 oz (150 g) regular sugar

7 oz (200 g) kosher salt

1 fennel bulb, with stalk and fronds, finely chopped

1 oz (30 g) black peppercorns, cracked

1¾ oz (50 g) toasted fennel seeds, ground

1½ oz (40 g) dill seed, toasted and ground

3 sprigs dill, chopped fine

½ cup (118 ml) brennivin (Icelandic liquor; can substitute sambuca)

2½ lb (1.1 kg) Artic char

Cheesecloth

Mix sugar and salt with chopped herbs and liquor. Position the fish skin side down. Mix spices and distribute evenly over flesh side of fish. Mix any leftover spices into salt and sugar mixture.

Lay out enough cheesecloth to wrap fish 4 times. Spread out 1 inch (2.5 cm) thick of the salt and sugar mixture at the front edge of cheesecloth. Position fish skin side down on this thick layer. Cover the entire flesh side of the fish with the remaining salt and sugar mix.

Wrap the fish as tightly as possible. Position in nonreactive (glass or plastic) pan and weight down with something heavy (weighing 5 lb [2 kg]) in refrigerator for 2 days. To test the doneness, push on the middle. If the fish feels firm, it's done. If it's still soft, let it cure for 12 additional hours.

Gently unwrap the fish, rinse off the salt and pat dry. The fish will keep in the refrigerator in plastic wrap for 3 weeks. If you are keeping it for more than 1 week, wrap the fish in butcher paper and change it every few days.

Serve the fish sliced with roast beets and dill crème-fraiche vinaigrette. Or slice thin and put on top of an "everything" bagel with cream cheese and raw onion. The fish also tastes great in Caesar salad. Tightly wrapped in plastic, it has about a week's shelf life.

Landjaeger

Yield: 15 sausages

The name landjaeger translates to "land soldier" and during World War II they'd give the soldiers these sausages, much like beef jerky. Growing up in Hartford, Connecticut, I remember seeing landjaeger hanging in a German market and snacking on very thin slices. Later, I'd buy and sample them whenever I saw them and found there are lots of different flavors, from beef or pork as the start to additions such as caraway seeds. I like pork, but you can substitute beef for this recipe, or half pork and half beef.

4½ lb (2 kg) pork meat

½ lb (225 g) fatback

¼ cup (59 ml) dry white wine

1½ oz (40 g) kosher salt

¼–½ oz (10 g) black pepper, coarsely ground

½ oz (15 g) dextrose

¼ oz (6 g) curing salt no. 2

1 tsp (5 g) garlic powder

2 tsp (10 g) whole caraway seed

3 tsp (15 g) Hungarian paprika

1 tsp (5 g) yellow mustard seed

1 tsp (5 g) coriander seed, toasted and ground

Hog casing, soaked in tepid water for 2 hours before use

Set up the meat grinder, all metal parts from the freezer. Grind pork meat and fatback on small (¼") plate into a bowl sitting on ice.

Mix wine and the rest of the ingredients.

Set up a standing mixer over ice with a paddle attachment. Use the paddle to mix the meat with the spice-and-wine mixture.

Soak the casing in tepid water for 2 hours to soften it before stuffing it. Keep the casing wet while you work with it. Slide the casing onto the funnel but don't make a knot. Put the mixture in the stuffer and pack it down. Begin extruding. As the mixture comes out, pull the casing back over the nozzle and tie a knot.

Extrude one full coil, about 48 inches (1.3 m) long, and tie it off. Crimp with fingers to separate sausages into 5-inch (10-cm) lengths. Twist the casing once one way, then the other way between each sausage link. Repeat along the entire coil. Once the sausage is cased, use a sterile needle to prick any air pockets. Prick each sausage 4 or 5 times. Repeat the casing process to use remaining sausage.

Select a cookie tray with sides that will accommodate all the sausages without stacking them. Line the tray with deli or wax paper, then lay all sausages side by side on the tray. Cover with waxed paper, press with a weight of 3–4 lb (1–1.5 kg) and put in the refrigerator for 36 hours.

Set the chips on fire using one pan, then smother them out with a small amount of water. Transfer the smoldering chips to the bottom half of a two-part perforated/nonperforated pan. Put the sausage in the top, then cover the pan tightly with tin foil. Poke 1 or 2 small holes in tin foil for smoke to escape. Cold smoke 2 hours.

Hang the sausages to cure 30 days in the refrigerator until firm throughout. If they are not firm after 30 days, hang them for 10 additional days. If using a curing room, set the temperature to 60°F–70°F (18°C–21°C) with 60% to 70% humidity. Sealed in plastic wrap, these sausages can be refrigerated for up to 6 months.

Tuna Bottarga

Yield: 1 (6- to 8-ounce [170- to 225-g]) piece

This is the simplest way to make bottarga (dried, pressed fish roe). You can make it with any type of roe. The cured fish, with its mild salty, fishy taste, is great on top of pasta or grilled vegetables. **Note:** I don't recommend using your everyday refrigerator for this recipe—use a dedicated refrigerator or a curing room.

½ cup (120 g) salt

¼ cup (60 g) sugar

1 (8-oz [227-g]) package fresh roe

2 tbsp (30 ml) olive oil

Cheesecloth

Mix the salt and sugar to combine. Toss the roe gently in the olive oil, then toss gently in the salt and sugar mixture. Cover a baking sheet with paper towels, then spread the roe out to drain.

Cover the sheet of roe lightly with plastic wrap and put the tuna in a cold, dry place—the refrigerator or an area below 50°F (10°C). The fish will be done curing at 5 to 7 days. At 5 days it will be crumbly, while at 7 days it will be firm.

Uncover the fish, brush off the salt, wrap in cheesecloth and age for 30 days.

Serve this tuna shaved or grated over pasta or on top of radishes with room temperature butter. It keeps in the refrigerator for about a month, though you can freeze it for up to a year.

Miso-Cured Pork Tenderloin

Yield: 1 (8 ounce [225 g]) pork tenderloin

We don't usually serve pork tenderloin in the restaurant since there are only two tenderloins per animal, and it doesn't really yield enough to serve multiple diners. I've experimented on my own, however, and the combination of natural salt in the miso and kombu (dried edible kelp) make a great cure. For variation, cold smoke the tenderloin ham and freeze it, then grate it over pasta or grilled vegetables like you would serve bottarga.

4 oz (113 g) kombu

½ lb (227 g) pork tenderloin

8 oz (227 g) white miso paste

½ cup (113 g) cracked black pepper

Soak kombu in water for 30 minutes. Towel dry the pork, then smear it with miso paste. Lay out kombu in a thin layer. Place pork on top. Roll up kombu and pork tenderloin like a canola. Wrap in plastic wrap, making sure it's air tight, then cure in the refrigerator for 14 days.

Once cured, brush off miso and throw away kombu. Roll in cracked black pepper and let sit in the refrigerator for 10 hours.

To serve this pork, slice and eat it like ham, use in stir-fry or soup, or grill and put on toast with butter. Wrapped in the refrigerator, it'll keep for up to 10 days.

American Country Ham (Do not try this at home.)

YIELD: 1 (12- TO 15-POUND [5.4- TO 6.8-KG]) HAM

Curing your own ham is very rewarding once you figure it out. Curing a ham means handling a lot of variables, and always handling the possibility of spoilage. If you're in doubt, throw it out—especially if your ham tastes or smells funny. The first few hams I made didn't work—so don't feel bad if you have mixed results. **Note:** Don't use your every-day refrigerator for making this ham—I recommend designating a refrigerator for curing or setting up a curing room. And remember this is not a 1-day recipe—you'll need 1–2 days for curing.

1 fresh back leg of pork, skin on, 15–20 lb (6.8–9.1 kg) (Have the butcher trim the leg for curing and remove the aitch (H) bone.)

5 lb (2 kg) salt

1 cup (235 ml) white wine diluted with ½ cup (118 ml) water

12 oz (341 g) cracked black pepper, ground medium fine

Using a mallet or rolling pin, hit the pork with good force in the middle of the leg. This will help drain residual blood in the femur artery. Hit the leg 15 to 20 times all over, then hang in a refrigerator overnight to let the blood drip into a pan.

Alternatively, place the leg in a nonreactive (glass or plastic) dish, skin side angled up, at a 35- to 40-degree angle for 1½ days.

Place the leg, skin side up, on a large sheet tray. Massage the salt into every part, starting with the exposed bone and then into the meat. Rub the salt generously, as if you're trying to exfoliate the leg.

Move the leg to a nonreactive (glass or plastic) pan, skin side up, and cover with 1 inch (2.5 cm) of salt. Let it cure in the refrigerator for 15 to 20 days (cure 1 day for every pound [450 g] of meat).

Check the leg every day. Reapply the salt if it's been absorbed or is falling off. Pour off any moisture.

When the ham is done, it will feel firm. If it's soft like a rare steak, then cure it an additional 3 to 5 days, adding salt as needed.

When it's done, wipe the salt off the ham, then wipe it down with wine to make it very dry. Rub the cracked pepper all over, skin and flesh sides.

Hang the ham in a dedicated refrigerator or curing room for 8 months (or up to 1 year). A smaller ham will take less time, and a larger ham will take longer. After 5 months use a hand tester to check the ham. If it smells like ham, it's done; if it smells like pork, it's not done. Don't use the hand tester before 5 months because it introduces oxygen into the meat by piercing the flesh.

While the ham is curing, check it frequently for black or green mold—if you see this, the ham must be thrown out. White mold, however, is okay. If you find fuzzy mold, you can make a mixture of 3 parts water, 1 part salt. Use a clean cloth and wipe off the ham, then wipe it dry with another clean cloth. If you've spotted fuzzy mold, check the ham frequently and rewipe as needed.

After the ham is done, cut off the skin. Carve the ham with a sharp knife, cutting slices as thin as possible. Make sure the hipbone is facing you, and carve toward yourself, only in one direction, parallel to the femur bone. This ham can be refrigerated, wrapped, for up to 6 months.

Ethiopian-Flavored Saucisson Sec

Yield: 15 sausages

I've been making Saucisson Sec for a long time. Years ago, I did a dinner with Marcus Samuelsson, an Ethiopian chef (he runs Harlem's Red Rooster). As I researched spices from his book to prepare for the dinner, I also did some experimenting. I ended up loving berbere and using it in so many recipes that my staff asked me to stop! The last thing I made before they banned it was this sausage. Berbere and baharat are very complex spice mixtures, and the combination gives this sausage a very floral North African flavor.

4½ lb (2 kg) pork meat

½ lb (225 g) fatback

1½ oz (40 g) kosher salt

¼ to ½ oz (10 g) black pepper, coarsely ground

½ oz (15 g) dextrose

¼ oz (6 g) curing salt no. 2

1 tsp (5 g) powdered garlic

2 tsp (10 g) berbere (Ethiopian spice mix)

1½ tsp (8 g) baharat

¼ cup (59 ml) water

Sheep or hog casing, soaked in tepid water for 2 hours before use

Set up the meat grinder, all metal parts from the freezer. Grind the pork meat and fatback on a large (¾" [1.9 cm]) plate into a bowl sitting on ice. Use a paddle to mix in all other ingredients.

Keep the casing wet while you work with it. Slide the casing onto the funnel but don't make a knot. Put the mixture in the stuffer and pack it down. Begin extruding. As the mixture comes out, pull the casing back over the nozzle and tie a knot.

Extrude one full coil, about 48 inches (1.3 m) long, and tie it off. Crimp with fingers to separate sausages into 12-inch (30-cm) lengths. Twist the casing once one way, then the other way between each sausage link. Repeat along the entire coil. Once the sausage is cased, use a sterile needle to prick any air pockets. Prick each sausage 4 or 5 times. Repeat the casing process to use remaining sausage.

Hang to cure for 18 to 20 days at 60°F–75°F (18°C–21°C).

You can refrigerate it in plastic wrap up for up to 6 months.

How to Make Money Off of Fatback: Lardo

Yield: 4 cups (950 ml)

Lardo, or pork butter, is an awesome alternative to butter. Using this basic recipe, you can make any number of flavored versions. The first recipe listed here makes a salty, savory, and sweet version that's perfect for bread or grilled vegetables. Recipes for black truffle honey butter and pepperoni-pizza-flavored lardo follow.

5 lb (2 kg) pork fat (any type, hard or soft, including lard or skin)

1 cup (237 ml) dry white wine

1 cup (237 ml) water

5 cloves garlic

1 fresh bay leaf

2 sprigs thyme

Salty /Savory /Sweet Version

1 tbsp (15 g) green curry

1 tbsp (15 g) sugar

1 tbsp (15 ml) lime juice

1 tsp (5 g) chopped garlic

2 tbsp (30 ml) fish sauce

1 tsp (5 g) coarse sea salt or fleur de sel

Black Truffle Honey Butter

1 tbsp (15 g) chopped rosemary

1 tbsp (15 ml) honey

2 tbsp (30 g) fresh, chopped black truffles

Pepperoni-Pizza-Flavored Lardo

1 tsp (15 g) smoked paprika

1 tsp (5 g) red chili flakes

1 tsp (5 g) granulated garlic

1 tsp (5 g) ground black pepper

1 tsp (15 ml) olive oil

1 tsp (5 g) sea salt

Cut the pork fat into 1-inch (2.5-cm) pieces. Use a crockpot or a very heavy-bottomed Dutch oven with a lid. Put everything in the pot.

If using a crockpot, cook 2 hours on high followed by 2 hours on low. If using a Dutch oven, cook on low, stirring every 10 to 15 minutes, for 3 to 4 hours.

Once the pork fat is cooked, strain it through a fine-mesh sieve. Place it in a casserole dish, press with a 3–4-lb (1–1.5-kg) weight and cool until it's firm like butter.

Salty/Savory/Sweet Version

Then put 2 cups (473 ml) in an electric mixer with a paddle attachment and add green curry, sugar, lime juice, garlic and fish sauce. (Reserve the other 2 cups [473 ml] for confit or other use). Cream until it resembles whipped butter, then transfer it to a dish until ready for serving.

Serve on grilled bread with fleur de sel.

Black Truffle Honey Butter

Once the pork fat is firm, put 2 cups (473 ml) in an electric mixer with a paddle attachment and add 1 tablespoon (15 g) chopped rosemary, 1 tablespoon (15 ml) honey, and 2 tablespoons (30 g) fresh, chopped black truffles. Cream until it's the consistency of whipped butter and transfer it to a dish for serving.

Pepperoni-Pizza-Flavored Lardo

Once the pork fat is firm, put 2 cups (473 ml) in an electric mixer with a paddle attachment and add 1 tablespoon (15 g) smoked paprika, 1 teaspoon (5 g) red chili flakes, 1 teaspoon (5 g) granulated garlic, 1 teaspoon (5 g) ground black pepper, 1 teaspoon (5 ml) olive oil and 1 teaspoon (5 g) sea salt. Cream until it's the consistency of whipped butter and transfer it to a dish for serving.

This butter can be refrigerated in plastic wrap for up to 6 months.

Chorizo Fresca (Breakfast, or Grilling, Sausage)

Yield: 15 to 20 sausages

The flavors you want in a breakfast sausage are different from those you want in a grilled sausage—if dinner sausage is savory, the breakfast version is sweet. To give this recipe a nod toward sweetness, I used powdered milk and dextrose. This gives it just enough sweetness without being overpowering but at the same time retains the sausage's handmade flavor.

10 lb (4 kg) pork butt

5 lb (2 kg) pork belly

¼ oz (7–10 g) cumin

¼ oz (7 g) fennel

¼ oz (7–10 g) coriander

2 cloves garlic

3½ oz (100 g) dextrose

½ oz (16 g) curing salt no. 2

3 oz (90 g) nonfat dairy milk powder

4 oz (113 g) kosher salt

4 oz (113 g) Hungarian paprika

4½ oz (134 g) smoked paprika de La Vera

1 (8-oz [4-g]) espelette

¼ oz (7–10 g) cascabel powder

½ oz (16 g) black pepper, fresh ground

1–1½ cups (237–356 ml) tepid water (to purée spices)

Canola oil

Hog casing, soaked in tepid water for 2 hours before use

Set up the meat grinder, all metal parts from the freezer. Grind the pork butt and belly back on a large (¾" [1.9 cm]) plate into a bowl sitting on ice.

Toast and grind cumin, fennel and coriander. Mix with all remaining ingredients and purée in a blender.

Heat up a small sauté pan with a little canola oil. Pull off a 1-inch (2.5-cm) piece of the pâté, fry and taste for seasoning. Adjust seasonings.

Keep the casing wet while you work with it. Slide the casing onto the funnel but don't make a knot. Put the mixture in the stuffer and pack it down. Begin extruding. As the mixture comes out, pull the casing back over the nozzle and tie a knot.

Extrude one full coil, about 48 inches (1.3 m) long, and tie it off. Crimp with fingers to separate sausages into 12-inch (30-cm) lengths. Twist the casing once one way, then the other way between each sausage link. Repeat along the entire coil. Once the sausage is cased, use a sterile needle to prick any air pockets. Prick each sausage 4 or 5 times. Repeat the casing process to use remaining sausage.

Hang the sausage to cure for 12 hours.

Grill to order or poach until internal temperature reaches 145°F (63°C). Cool, cut in half and grill. It can keep, cooked, for 6 days in the refrigerator.

LARDO

YIELD: 1 (4-POUND [1.8-KG]) PIECE OF LARDO

There are lots and lots of recipes for lardo, also known as white prosciutto. Traditional Italian recipes use marble boxes for processing lardo because any light will cause the fat to oxidize and break down. The resulting mix will have a yellow color and taste mildewy. If you're worried at all about oxidation, or the lardo tastes off, don't take a chance—throw it out and try again.

4 lb (1.8 kg) pork fatback, skin on, as thick as possible

FOR THE CURE

½ cup (120 g) kosher salt

1½ tbsp (25 g) powdered dextrose

1 tsp (5 g) curing salt no. 2

2 tbsp (30 g) espelette chili flakes

½ tbsp (7 g) black pepper

2 bunches fresh thyme

10 fresh bay leaves

3 cups (710 ml) white wine

Cheesecloth

Mix all ingredients for the cure. In a nonreactive (glass or plastic) dish, massage the cure into the fat and skin.

Place the fat in a container with no light, such as a Dutch oven (not glass). Distribute thyme and bay leaves on top, cover with tin foil, press with a 5-pound (2-kg) weight and refrigerate for 2 days.

After 2 days, flip out and using a wooden spoon, mix with white wine. Cover, then let sit in refrigerator for 18 days.

When it's done, pat dry, wrap in cheesecloth, tie tightly, and hang for 7 to 14 days. (The lardo is ready at 7 days, but you can age it for up to 2 weeks.)

Unwrap, slice and serve the lardo like prosciutto. Alternatively, cut it into 1-pound (450-g) pieces, wrap it in plastic wrap, and freeze it until it's ready for use. This can be wrapped and refrigerated for a couple of months.

Boquerones

Yield: About ½ pound (225 g) of boquerones

I was travelling in Spain the first time I saw a white anchovy. After sampling it, I fell in love with the bright, vinegary flavor. After doing some research, I learned that white and black anchovy are the same fish, but they're processed differently. A lot of the white anchovy I sampled was dry, so I set out to develop a recipe with bright flavor and moist texture. (Black anchovy, by the way, is salt-cured, giving it a salty, fishy flavor.)

½ lb (227 g) fresh anchovies

¼ cup (60 g) kosher salt

3 cups (710 ml) white wine vinegar

5 cloves garlic, sliced

¼ cup (79 ml) extra virgin olive oil

Clean the anchovies (or have them cleaned) so they are eviscerated, bellies split and guts removed.

Season the fish with salt only and place in a nonreactive (glass or plastic) pan. Cover the fish with vinegar and let sit in the refrigerator for 18 hours.

Remove fish from the pan and dry on a towel. Using a sharp knife, cut the fillets of fish off the bone. Discard the vinegar and wash out the pan.

Put the fish back in the pan, skin side down. Scatter the sliced garlic over the top and cover with olive oil. Cover and let sit 2 days in the refrigerator. They'll keep for up to a month in oil.

Bologna

YIELD: ONE 8-LB (3.6-KG) BOLOGNA

When I was growing up I loved bologna. That is, until I learned that bologna is basically the American word for "poorly made sausage from Bologna." So I set out to make my own version of this classic. I think bologna is best served on its own, either cut into cubes or sliced. This will keep in the fridge for 3-4 weeks.

3 lbs (1.3 kg) pork belly, rind on, diced to ½" x ½" (1.3 cm x 1.3 cm) pieces & kept cold

4.5 lbs (2 kg) pork butt, diced to ½" x ½" (1.3 x 1.3 cm) pieces & kept cold

½ cup (118g) dextrose

3 tsp (15 g) TCM #1 (Prague powder)

1.5 lbs (600 g) ice, kept solid

½ cup (125 g) salt

4 tbsp (60 g) cayenne

Canola oil

1 lb (0.45 kg) fatback, diced and blanched

1–1.5 lbs (0.45 to 0.6 kg) pistachios, toasted whole and cooled

3 cups (700 g) whole black peppercorns

Beef bung, soaked in tepid water for 2 hours before use

Set up the meat grinder, all metal parts from the freezer. Combine pork belly, pork butt, dextrose, and Prague powder.

Grind on the small (⅛") plate into a bowl sitting on ice. Add 1½ pounds (680 g) of ice and grind again. Repeat process until emulsified, continuing to work over ice.

Season with salt and cayenne to taste.

Heat up a small sauté pan with a little canola oil. Pull off a 1- to 2-inch (1.3–2.5-cm) piece and fry in a saucepan, then taste for seasoning. Adjust seasonings as needed. Fold in chilled fatback, toasted pistachios and the peppercorns.

Keep the beef bung wet while you work with it. Slide the casing onto the funnel but don't make a knot. Put the meat in the stuffer and pack it down. Begin extruding. As the meat comes out, pull the casing back over the nozzle and tie a knot.

Extrude one full coil, about 48 inches (1.3 m) long, and tie it off. Crimp with fingers to separate sausage. Twist the casing once one way, then the other way in between sausage links. Repeat along the entire coil. Once the sausage is cased, use a sterile needle to prick any air pockets. Prick each sausage 4 or 5 times.

Repeat the casing process to use remaining sausage. Alternatively, wrap in plastic. Poach until the sausage reaches an internal temperature of 150°F (65°C), then cool on a rack to serve. Slice thin to serve, removing beef bung if using.

Chapter Four

Confit and Fat

When you're working with whole animals, you'll cook with their fat. The word "confit" comes from the French word confire, which means "to prepare." All of these recipes are slowly cooked in—you guessed it—fat. Most of these recipes have a six-day shelf life, sealed in the refrigerator.

Turkey Hash

Feeds 10 to 15 people

One of my favorite places for corned beef hash is Mike's City Diner next to Toro in Boston. I wanted to make a version of hash using turkey (as I've said, I love turkey), and after a lot of research I arrived at this recipe. It's great for breakfast, lunch or dinner. Deliciously smoky from paprika, it's the perfect greasy breakfast dish.

1 cup (240 g) salt

½ cup (120 g) sugar

1 tsp (5 g) ground black peppercorns

1 tsp (5 g) smoked paprika

1 tsp (5 g) ground coriander

2 turkey legs, 2 lb (900 g) each

1 gal (3.8 l) duck fat or lard

3 cloves garlic, minced

2 white or Spanish onions, diced

1 red bell pepper, diced

3 Idaho potatoes, peeled and diced large

2 sprigs tarragon, picked and chopped

1 tsp (5 ml) Tabasco sauce

1 tbsp (15 ml) Worcestershire sauce

Mix salt and sugar with dry spices. Rub the turkey legs and lightly cure for 10 minutes at room temperature.

Bring the fat to 200°F (93°C). Once the fat is rendered, place the turkey legs in a large pan and pour the fat over the legs. Cover with tin foil, place in 200°F (93°C) oven, and let the turkey legs simmer for 3 hours.

Remove a small amount of fat and place in a sauté pan. Cook garlic and onion until tender, then add red pepper.

In a separate pan, cover the diced potatoes with fat; use about 3 cups (710 ml), or just enough to cover the potatoes. Cook until just tender, 10 to 15 minutes at just below a simmer. Then strain the fat and place the potatoes in a bowl with the cooked garlic mixture and tarragon.

Pick the turkey clean; tear the meat into 1- to 1½-inch (2.5–3.7-cm) chunks. Discard the bone and skin. Mix the turkey and the potato mix, add Tabasco and Worcestershire sauce, and adjust seasonings with salt and pepper as needed.

Chill until cool. Cook immediately or store for several days in the refrigerator. To cook, form 4-inch (10-cm) patties. Heat vegetable oil in a nonstick or cast-iron pan and cook the patties until golden brown on both sides and hot throughout.

Chicken Wings with Honey and Za'atar

Feeds 4 to 6 people

When I was growing up, chicken wings were one of my favorite things to eat. My mom wasn't that good a cook, but I loved her barbecue honey chicken wings. As an adult, I find them far too sweet, however, so I set out to make my own version of her recipe. I love the combination of honey and za'atar—the za'atar adds a slightly acidic tanginess that works great with the urfa pepper.

1 lb (450 g) chicken wings

1 tbsp (15 g) salt

1½ tsp (8 g) black pepper

8 cups (1.9 l) Schmaltz (or duck fat or lard, see page 151)

2 cups (473 ml) honey

4 tbsp (60 ml) white wine vinegar (preferably chardonnay)

1 tsp (5 g) urfa pepper

4 tbsp (60 g) za'atar

1 tbsp (15 g) toasted sesame seeds

Sea salt

Sliced chives

Season the wings with salt and pepper. Bring the fat to 200°F (93°C) over a simmer. Once the fat is rendered, place chicken wings in a large pan and the pour fat over the wings. Cover with tin foil, place in 200°F (93°C) oven, and let simmer for 1 hour and 20 minutes.

Cool the wings in an in ice bath to room temperature. Remove them from the fat and let them dry on a wire rack. (The wings can be stored in fat in the refrigerator for up to 2 weeks.)

Mix the honey, vinegar, urfa and za'atar until combined.

Roast chicken wings in a 400°F (204°C) oven for 12 minutes or until brown and golden.

When the wings are done, place them on a serving tray and drizzle with honey glaze, then sprinkle with sesame seeds, sea salt and chives.

Grilled Pig Tails

Feeds 4 to 6 people

I've always loved pork ribs, but ribs tend to be very expensive. Although most people don't know it, a pig's tail muscle structure goes up its back 3 to 4 inches (7.6–10 cm). This area contains a lot of luscious meat and fat. Pig's tails are an inexpensive but very tasty cut of meat—and a great-tasting alternative to ribs.

1 cup (240 g) salt

½ cup (120 g) sugar

1 tsp (5 g) mustard seed

1 tsp (5 g) whole coriander

1 tsp (5 g) fennel seeds

1 tsp (5 g) black peppercorns

1 lb (450 g) pig's tails

8 cups (1.9 l) Schmaltz (or duck fat or lard; see page 151)

Mix together salt, sugar and spices. Coat the pig's tails and place them in the refrigerator for 6 hours to cure. Submerge the tails in water to rinse, then pat them dry. Place the tails in a large pan.

Bring fat to 200°F (93°C) over a simmer. Once the fat is rendered, pour it over the tails. Cover with tin foil, place in 200°F (93°C) oven, and cook for 8 to 12 hours. Tails are done when the meat is tender; to test, fold tails in half. When the tails are done, they will break without resistance.

Remove the pan from the oven and place the entire pan in an ice bath to cool. The tails can be stored in the fat for 1 to 2 weeks. If removing the tails from the fat, let drip dry. Cook on a hot grill or sauté in a cast-iron grill pan. If grilling, use medium heat and cook the tails until they are caramelized and hot. Serve with Mostarda (see recipe, page 136).

Coppa di Testa

Yield: 2 pounds (900 g)

Coppa is one of my favorite dishes to make—I really love the flavor and texture of cooked pig's head. Honestly, this 2-day recipe is named as such so I can serve pig's head in the restaurant without having to call it pig's head!

1 pig's head (8-11 lb [3-4 kg])

2 lb (900 g) mirepoix, wrapped in cheesecloth

1 small sachet containing 1 tsp (5 g) each: black peppercorn, coriander, fennel seeds, mustard seeds, garlic, tarragon, thyme and juniper

1 bottle of white wine

1 tbsp + 1 tsp (20 g) thyme, chopped

1 tbsp (15 g) rosemary, chopped

2 tbsp (30 g) esplette

4 ½ tbsp (70 g) black pepper

¼ oz (7-10 g) chili flakes

1 tbsp plus 1 tsp (20 g) sweet paprika

4 tbsp (60 ml) extra-virgin olive oil

¼ oz (7-10 g) fennel pollen (or fennel seed)

For the brine

1 gallon (3.8 L) water

¾ cup (180 g) kosher salt

¾ cup (180 g) sugar

For the brine, warm water to 100°F (37.7°C), dissolve salt and sugar and then cool.

Cover the pig's head with cold water and let it sit at room temperature for 8 hours or in the walk-in refrigerator overnight. Put the pig's head into the brine and let sit for 3 days. Strain the liquid off and discard.

Place the pig's head into a pot large enough to cover with water that is 6 inches (15 cm) higher than the pig's head. Add mirepoix, sachet and wine to pot.

Bring to a boil and skim, then lower to a simmer and let cook, uncovered, for 6 to 8 hours. Strain, saving the liquid and the head. Discard the sachet and mirepoix.

Reduce the poaching liquid rapidly, skimming and clarifying as needed.

When the head is cool enough to handle but still warm, pick the meat from the skull. Cut skin, fat and meat into large dice and allow to cool. Season with herbs, espelette pepper and black pepper.

Mix spices with reduced liquid. Rub mason jars witih olive oil so the meat doesn't stick. Pour spiced liquid into a mason jar lined with plastic wrap. Pack the meat 1 inch (2.5 cm) at a time to avoid air holes. Pack the meat in the liquid in the jar until the jar is ¾ full, then cover with plastic wrap and use another jar to lightly press the top. Cool in the refrigerator overnight.

When the coppa is cold, unmold it and remove the plastic wrap. Slice the coppa ¼-inch thick and serve it with Salsa Verde (see recipe, page 147).

Vietnamese Fried Bones

Feeds 6 to 8 people

When I was in Vietnam, I saw a lot of pig roasts. After the pork was eaten, people would save the bones, then later fry them and serve them with Nuoc Cham (see recipe, page 149). In the same way that we eat spare ribs, these bones are very flavorful and great finger food. Before you start on this recipe, make sure you have 2 gallons of Dashi (see recipe, page 150). After you've first cooked the bones, you'll have a batch of wonderful stock—this can be used for braising or poaching sausage or as a base for soup.

5 lb (2 kg) mixed pork bones (with meat attached)

Kosher salt

2 gal (7.6 l) Dashi (page 150)

2 cups (480 g) rice flour (can substitute regular flour)

Vegetable oil for frying

2 cups (480 g) mint, picked and chopped

2 cups (480 g) Thai basil, picked and chopped

3 cups (720 g) cilantro, washed but not picked, chopped with stems intact

¼ cup (60 g) fried garlic (can be purchased in an Asian supermarket)

2 cups (480 g) toasted chopped peanuts

2 cups (480 g) fresh bean stems

1½ cups (355 ml) Nuoc Cham (page 149)

Salt for seasoning

Pepper for seasoning

Dust the bones with kosher salt and let them sit for 4 hours. In a large pot, cover the bones with dashi and bring to a simmer. Turn to a low simmer and let cook 90 minutes or until you can pull the meat off the bones.

Strain the stock and set aside. Let the bones dry on a roasting pan in the refrigerator for up to 3 days.

Dredge the bones in rice flour, then deep-fry in vegetable oil heated to 375°F (190°C). Fry 3 to 5 minutes until hot and crispy. Place the bones in the bottom of a casserole dish for serving. Cover with herbs, peanuts and bean stems, then pour nuoc cham on top. Season with salt and pepper if needed.

Foie Gras Torchon

Yield: 2 torchons

This is one of the best cold preparations for foie gras. I read about it for years, then I tried Ken Oringer's version. I modified his recipe after I found that poaching the foie gras in duck fat, then cooling it, makes this a very easy 2-day recipe. He cooks it in fat, not stock, which prevents oxidization. It tastes brighter.

2 lb (900 g) foie gras, A grade

Seltzer water

3 tsp (15 g) salt

2 tsp (10 g) sugar

2 tsp (10 g) curing salt no. 1

2 tsp (10 g) ground white pepper

1 tsp (5 g) ground nutmeg

2 tbsp (30 ml) green chartreuse liquor

1 gal (3.8 l) duck fat or lard

Fleur de sel, to taste

Green Tomato Chutney (page 138)

Cheesecloth

Butcher's twine

Temper and clean the foie gras: Soak foie gras in seltzer water. Let it warm up to room temperature so it's pliable.

Open up the lobes and pull out the veins or arteries. Line a tray with parchment paper. Press through a tamis (very-fine-mesh sieve) onto the tray.

Mix salt, sugar, curing salt, white pepper and nutmeg. Sprinkle evenly over the foie gras, then drizzle with green chartreuse liquor. Mix to combine.

Roll the foie gras into four 8-ounce (227-g) rolls about 2 inches (5 cm) in diameter and 6 to 7 inches (15–18 cm) long. Roll it in parchment paper, then wrap it in plastic wrap and tie the ends. Hang in refrigerator or curing room overnight.

The next day, gently unwrap. Rewrap in cheesecloth 8 times, then tie very tightly on ends using butcher's twine. Tie 1 strip of cheesecloth in the middle, plus 1 on each side, to hold it tightly without cracking it.

Put in a nonreactive (glass or plastic) container. Warm the duck fat to 120°F (49°C), then pour it over the foie gras. Put it in the refrigerator to cool for 24 hours. When it's done, gently scrape off the duck fat and pull out torchons.

Cut off cheesecloth, then reroll in airtight plastic wrap. When the foie gras is ready to serve, slice it cold, season it with fleur de sel and top with green tomato chutney.

Chapter Five

Hoof and Snout Mafia

Charcuterie works with the whole animal, cooking and cutting and seasoning it. That means brains, kidneys, glands. This isn't something you should rush: These recipes take some finesse. But it's enormously fun to take an ingredient that might not be pretty to look at and turn it into something great. Is a heart "pretty"? No. So it's nice to turn it into something precious and fun. I love the irony behind it. Unless otherwise noted, these dishes can keep in the refrigerator for 6 days, wrapped.

Tripe à la Collinsville

Yield: 6 pounds (2.7 kg) of tripe

When it comes to cooking, roasting a chicken is easy. To me, the true sign of a good cook is one who can take something that looks and smells terrible and make it taste good. Tripe is one of those ingredients. As a young cook, I noticed that traditional recipes would often be named for the chef's place of origin or the ingredient's place of origin. After I made this recipe for tripe, I gave a traditional nod to the town where I grew up—Collinsville, Connecticut, population 800.

10 lb (4 kg) honeycomb tripe

4 cups (0 .95 l) white wine

2 cups (473 g) white wine

1 cup (240 g) salt

1 gal (3.8 l) chicken stock, or enough to cover tripe by 4" (10 cm)

Small sachet with 1 tsp (5 g) each: caraway, coriander, fennel seed and mustard seed

For the Stew

20 shallots, julienned

4 tbsp (60 ml) extra-virgin olive oil

10 garlic cloves, sliced

4 Anaheim peppers, julienned

4 poblano peppers, julienned

2 red jalapeño peppers, julienned

1 fennel bulb, brunoise

5 cups (1.2 l) apple jack whiskey

One #10 can 74/40 tomatoes, or 4 lb (1.5 kg) mixed heirloom tomatoes, chopped, skin on, seeds in

Salt and espelette pepper to taste

If the tripe is frozen, defrost it in cold water in the refrigerator. Soak it in water with 4 cups (945 ml) white wine for 3 to 12 hours.

Discard the water and whiten and clean the tripe by scrubbing with the blunt side of a French knife. Rinse, then cover again in a pot of cold water with 2 cups (473 ml) white wine and 1 cup (227 g) salt.

Bring to a simmer. Turn off immediately and strain. Return the tripe to the pot, and cover it by 4 inches (10 cm) chicken stock. Add sachet. Bring to boil, reduce to low simmer, cover with tight-fitting lid and cook for 5 to 6 hours.

Cool the tripe overnight in its liquid (if possible, cool it in a metal container set in ice so it will be easier to heat again).

For the Stew

Sweat shallots in olive oil in a tall stockpot.

While cooking shallots, bring the tripe back to a boil, then strain it, reserving braising liquid. When the shallots are tender, add garlic and cook until translucent. Add all three peppers and fennel. Cook until tender.

Add the strained tripe, sachet and apple jack. Reduce by half. Strain and dice the 74/40 or heirloom tomatoes. Add tomato pulp and reduce to simmer. Cook for 45 minutes, rewetting with tripe-braising liquid as needed. Thin to desired consistency with tripe liquid.

Finish with salt and espelette. This tripe will keep, if cooled properly, for 7 to 10 days in the refrigerator.

To serve, season with herbs fines, lemon and butter.

Pig's Foot Parmesan

Feeds 2 people

Because we cook with whole animals, we often end up with a lot of pig's feet. You can substitute any slow-cooked pork here but I love the flavor of pig's feet and they're under $1 each. The recipe takes time but they are very flavorful. For variation, cut the cutlets into breadstick-like pieces and serve as an appetizer.

1 lb (450 g) mirepoix

1 bulb fennel, chopped

3 cloves garlic, minced

Vegetable oil

3 cups (710 ml) dry white wine

2 gal (7.6 l) chicken stock

Lard or vegetable oil for panfrying

2 pig's feet, about 1 lb (450 g) each

For the Herb Bunch

2 fresh bay leaves

2 sprigs thyme

2 sprigs tarragon

1 sprig rosemary

For Dredging

4 cups (960 g) flour

8 eggs, beaten

4 cups (960 g) fine bread crumbs

For Garnish

4 cups (0.95 l) marinara sauce

12 oz (340 g) fresh mozzarella cheese (approx. 3 oz [85 g] per pig's foot cutlet)

1 cup (240 g) fresh grated Parmesan cheese

Olive oil

¼ cup (60 g) chopped parsley

¼ cup (60 g) chopped mint

Cook the mirepoix, fennel and garlic in vegetable oil until caramelized. When it's tender, add pig's feet, herb bunch and wine and cook out wine, about 3 minutes. Add chicken stock, cover tightly, and cook in 300°F (149°C) oven. Cook the feet for 3 to 5 hours or until the meat pulls away from the bone.

Remove the feet from the oven and cool them to room temperature. Place the pig's feet on a cooking sheet. Butterfly open and remove all bones. Cool meat in the refrigerator until cold.

Cut each foot in half. Combine dredging ingredients in a large bowl. Dip in flour, then egg, then bread crumbs, then repeat with just egg and bread crumbs (To remember this, think "FEBEB.")

Panfry the cutlets in lard or vegetable oil until golden brown. Put them on a baking sheet, then top them with marinara sauce and mozzarella and bake for 12 minutes at 375°F (190°C). Put them on a platter, sprinkle with Parmesan cheese, drizzle with olive oil and sprinkle chopped parsley and mint on top.

Bone Marrow and Oxtail

Feeds 4 to 6 people

At first glance this recipe looks daunting—but once you make it, you'll see that the time is truly worth the effort. The bone marrow has a very rich, beefy taste. When you combine that with the sweet and salty taste of the oxtail marmalade, it's delicious.

5 lb (2 kg) oxtail

Salt to taste

Pepper to taste

1 lb (450 g) mirepoix

1 stick lemongrass, chopped

5 cloves garlic

Small sachet of 1 tsp (5 g) each: star anise, cinnamon, fennel, coriander

2 cups (473 ml) red wine

2 gal (7.6 l) Dashi (page 150)

3 tbsp (45 ml) soy sauce

2 tbsp (30 ml) fish sauce

4 tbsp (60 g) sugar

8 pieces bone marrow, cut lengthwise, about 6" (15 cm) long

Sea salt

Black pepper

Sliced white bread

Espelette chili flakes

Chives

Salt and pepper the oxtail, then dry roast it in a 350°F (176°C) oven for 1 hour. Turn every 15 minutes.

Pour rendered fat into a pan and cook mirepoix, lemongrass and garlic until tender. Add sachet, oxtail and red wine.

Add dashi and bring to a boil. Once it boils, put a lid on it and place it in a 350°F (176°C) oven for 2½ hours until tender. When it's done, let it cool to room temperature.

Pick the meat from the bones OR transfer it to a nonreactive (glass or plastic) pan and let it sit overnight in the refrigerator. The next day, gently warm the stock and pick the meat from the bones. Discard bones. Set aside the meat.

Reduce 4 cups (0.95 l) stock to 1 cup (237 ml). Shred the meat and add it to reduced stock. Add soy sauce, fish sauce and sugar. Stir and cook until mixture resembles marmalade.

Set aside or cool and warm later. Oxtail marmalade will last in refrigerator 1 week.

Soak the bone marrow in water with a pinch of salt until ready to use. Preheat the oven to 400°F (204°C). Season the bone marrow with salt and pepper, then place it cut side down on a roasting pan and bake 8 minutes. Remove bone marrow from the pan and place sliced bread into rendered fat. Place the bone marrow back on top of the bread (2 pieces of bread per piece of marrow). Cook 6 minutes or until the internal temperature of the bone marrow reaches 140°F (60°C).

When the bone marrow is done, put it on a tray. Season it with sea salt, black pepper, espelette chili flakes and chives. Flip bread onto a plate, toasted side up. Top the bread with oxtail marmalade. Pair it with fresh radishes and pickled citrus.

Texas BBQ Kidney

Feeds 4 to 6 people

For years I would cook kidneys and bury them in a larger recipe so you couldn't taste them. But after I tried a recipe from a friend's cookbook and liked it, I realized it wasn't the kidneys I didn't like; it was the way I cooked them! This is an easy and very tasty 2-day recipe based on the teachings of Tremont 647 chef Andy Husbands. They taste like a really good, sweet barbecue, with a bit of tanginess.

1 lb (450 g) pork kidney

Milk

1 gal (3.8 l) chicken stock

1 onion, chopped rough

1 carrot, chopped rough

8 cloves garlic, chopped rough

Vegetable oil

1 small red pepper, diced small

1 cup (237 ml) ketchup

3 tbsp (45 ml) whole-grain mustard

1 tbsp (15 ml) Dijon mustard

3 tbsp (45 ml) sorghum molasses

2 tbsp (30 g) yellow madras curry

2 tbsp (30 g) spicy smoked paprika

Salt

Pepper

Tabasco sauce

Soak the kidney in milk overnight. The next day, cover it with chicken stock and simmer until just tender, 45 to 60 minutes.

Set up the meat grinder, all metal parts from the freezer. While the cooked kidney is still warm, grind the meat on a medium-size (¼") plate into a bowl sitting on ice. Grind it a second time. Strain, then reserve liquid.

Grind chopped onion, carrot and garlic through same grinder. Mix ground meat with ground vegetables. Sauté ground mixture in vegetable oil until cooked through.

Add red pepper, ketchup, mustards, molasses, curry and paprika. Cook until the consistency resembles Sloppy Joes. If it sticks, add a small amount of reserved liquid, 1 tablespoon (15 ml) at a time.

Taste, adjust seasonings with salt, pepper and Tabasco sauce. Serve on miniature potato rolls.

Veal Brains Piccata

Feeds 4 to 6 people

Growing up in the 1980s, I loved the flavors of piccata, a classic Italian dish made from sautéed veal or chicken served with a sauce made with lemon juice and capers. Because piccata is easy to make and veal brains cook quickly, I combined the two for a fast and delicious recipe.

1 lb (450 g) veal brains

Milk for soaking (if using fresh brains)

Salt

Pepper

Flour for dredging

¾ cup (180 g) clarified butter

1 tbsp (15 g) whole butter

1 tsp (5 g) capers

1 lemon, sliced

For the Court Bouillon

3 oz (85 g) Spanish onion, diced

2 oz (57 g) carrot, diced

2 oz (57 g) celery, diced

1 oz (30 g) garlic, crushed

½ oz (14 g) fennel seed

½ oz (14 g) coriander seed

½ oz (14 g) black peppercorns

½ oz (14 g) mustard seed

½ oz (14 g) paprika

1 gal (3.8 l) water

2 cups (473 ml) Grunter Veltliner (white wine)

3 oz (85 g) kosher salt

For the Garnish

Bergamot zest, chopped very fine

Bergamot oil

If the veal brains are frozen, thaw them in the packaging. If fresh, soak in milk for 1 hour.

Combine all ingredients for the court bouillon in a large pot and bring to a boil. Turn down and simmer for 10 minutes on low heat. Strain.

Bring the strained court bouillon back to a boil, then reduce to low simmer. Plunge the brains into the bouillon and cook just under a simmer for 8 minutes. Remove them to a tray lined with cloth, and let them cool in the refrigerator.

Cut the brains into 3-ounce (85-g) portions. Season with salt and pepper. Dredge in flour. Panfry in clarified butter. Brown on one side, then flip. Add whole butter and capers, then baste. Finish with lemon segments.

Plate the brains on a warm plate and garnish with capers from the pan, the cooked brown butter, lemon slices, bergamot zest and bergamot oil. They can keep refrigerated for up to 3 days.

Sweetbread Saltimbocca

Feeds 6 to 8 people

Growing up I always loved saltimbocca, which translates to "jumps in the mouth." It's usually made with veal, prosciutto and sage, sometimes brined, and often served with capers. I think regular old veal can be boring, so I substituted rich sweetbreads for this 2-day recipe. The sweetbreads add much more flavor and texture when cooked properly.

2 lb (900 g) sweetbreads

Milk

Salt

Pepper

16 sage leaves

4 oz (113 g) sliced prosciutto

¼ cup (60 g) flour

Canola oil

12 oz (340 g) wild mushrooms, cleaned

2 shallots, chopped

3 cloves garlic, minced

1 sprig thyme, picked and minced

½ cup (118 ml) Basque cider

2 tbsp (30 ml) sherry vinegar

4 tbsp (60 g) butter

For the Court Bullion

1 onion

1 rib celery

1 carrot

2 cloves garlic

3 sprigs thyme

2 fresh bay leaves

2 tbsp (30 g) Spanish paprika

1 tbsp (15 g) salt

1 gal (3.8 l) water

1 cup (237 ml) white wine

Vin santo for garnish

Soak sweetbreads overnight in milk. The next day, drain and pat dry.

Combine all ingredients for the court bullion and bring to a boil, then turn down to simmer. Put in sweetbreads, turn to just below a simmer and poach for 8 minutes.

Strain and discard the court bullion. Cool the sweetbreads on a tray lined with towels. Cover with a clean towel and press with a 2-pound (900-g) weight, such as cans of tomato sauce. Peel off the outer membrane and cut into 2-ounce (57-g) portions.

Season with salt and pepper. Put on one sage leaf, then wrap with prosciutto. Dust sweetbreads with flour, then sauté in canola oil. Panfry on both sides until golden brown. Remove, place on a tray and roast in 325°F (163°C) oven for 8 minutes.

While the sweetbreads are in the oven, add a small amount of oil to the sauté pan, then add mushrooms, shallots, garlic and thyme. Deglaze with Basque cider, then add sherry vinegar. Season with salt and pepper and finish with butter.

Serve sweetbreads on a platter with sauce on top. Garnish with drizzled vin santo. These keep in the refrigerator for up to 3 days.

Liver, Heart and Kidney Tacos

Feeds 4 to 6 people

Here's a simple rule of charcuterie: When you're dealing with things that people are afraid to eat, tacos are the way to go. Hence this 2-day recipe for livers, heart and kidney. You can use any kind of liver, heart and kidneys for this recipe—the method is the same—but I used chicken here, since these organ meats are widely available.

Equal parts, 4 oz (113 g) each: chicken liver, heart and kidneys

2 tomatillos, about the size of golf balls

1 tomato

3 oz (85 g) dried Mexican chili peppers

1 red onion

1 jalapeño pepper

¼ bunch (3 oz) cilantro, chopped but not picked

2 cloves garlic, minced

3 limes

Pepper, to taste

1 tbsp (15 ml) vegetable oil

12 oz (340 g) fresh corn tortilla

8 oz (228 g) radishes, sliced

1 white onion, diced small

Sea salt

Set up the meat grinder, all metal parts from the freezer. Grind the liver, heart and kidney on a medium-size (¼") plate into a bowl sitting on ice. Mix the meat to combine.

Cut the tomatillo and tomato in half. In a cast-iron pan, cook each half dry until charred black. Remove them, put them in a bowl and cover tightly with plastic wrap to steam. Cut the red onion in half, then char and steam the same way. Char the jalapeño on all sides, then wrap in plastic to steam.

For tomatillo, tomato and jalapeño, scrape off all black matter and seeds and discard. Chop the charred onion.

In a blender, combine half of cilantro, garlic and charred tomatillo, tomato and red onion. Squeeze in juice of 3 limes and blend until liquefied to make salsa. Season with sea salt and pepper to taste. Set aside.

In a cast-iron pan with vegetable oil, cook off the ground meats. Remove and discard the seeds of the dried Mexican pepper, then chop the pepper and add to meats while cooking. Add ½ of puréed salsa to the meat while it's cooking. Add water if needed. Cook until the dried pepper is tender. Season with salt, pepper, lime juice and salsa to taste.

Lightly oil a nonstick pan. To warm up tortillas, lightly dampen them on one side, then put the damp side down in the pan and cook on low heat.

To serve, assemble each tortilla on a large platter with 2 tablespoons (15 ml) meat mixture in the middle and topped with salsa and chopped cilantro. Scatter sliced radishes and diced white onion around the platter.

Pig Ear Terrine

Yield: 1 mold

I've always loved this dish, but it's taken me several years to perfect this easy and delicious 2-day recipe. With its mosaic layers of dark brown, black and white, this terrine looks beautiful displayed on a platter. This recipe will keep for 10 days in a cold walk-in refrigerator.

25 pig ears

Kosher salt

3 quarts (2.8 l) chicken or pork stock

3 cups (710 ml) soy sauce

2 cups (473 ml) mirin

1 cup (237 ml) sake

1 cup (237 ml) lemon or Meyer lemon simple syrup

Fleur de sel

2 cloves garlic, minced & fried

Fresh chives, snipped

For the Sachet

1 stalk lemon grass, chopped

2 pieces crystallized ginger

1 Fresno chili

1 tbsp (15 g) coriander, toasted

1 tbsp (15 g) grains of paradise

1 tbsp (15 g) fennel seed

4 cloves garlic

For the Garnish

Mini red shiso leaves

Ground sumac

Clean the pig ears of any hair. Lay them in a 4-inch (10.2-cm) hotel pan with the sachet in the middle. Season them gently with kosher salt.

Put the chicken stock, soy, mirin, sake and simple syrup into a saucepot and bring to a simmer. Pour the hot liquid over the ears, making sure the liquid covers the ears by ½ inch (1.2 cm). Cover tightly with plastic wrap, then with aluminum foil. Cook in a 200°F (93°C) oven for 36 hours. Check periodically that ears do not boil.

After 30 to 32 hours, check the pig ears with tweezers. They are done when the ears just fall to pieces but don't shred. The cartilage should be just past al dente.

Cool the ears in the liquid to room temperature, then remove them from the liquid. Reduce the liquid separately by ⅓. Layer the ears in a terrine mold lined with plastic wrap. Bring the meat ⅛ inch (0.3 cm) from the top of the mold. Pour the liquid and shake the mold to cover the ears. Fold plastic wrap over the top to seal. Press with a 2-pound (900-g) weight in the refrigerator overnight.

Unmold the terrine, change the plastic wrap, and store the terrine in a cool place until ready to serve.

To serve the ears, cut them ¼ inch (6 mm) thick with a hot, wet knife. Season them with fleur de sel, fried garlic and snipped chives. At the restaurant we serve ours with a yuzu aioli, though any creamy and sour sauce would work well. Garnish with mini red shiso leaves and ground sumac.

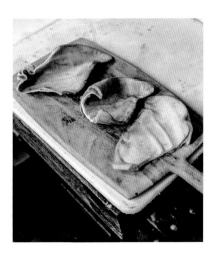

Chapter six

Something on the Side

These are sauces, sides and accoutrements that go well with charcuterie. When you're cooking this stuff, at least one or all of these sauces will taste good. It's also a way to get even more creative and resourceful, because many of these use leftover animal pieces. Unless indicated otherwise, these recipes keep sealed and refrigerated for about a month.

MOSTARDA

YIELD: 2 QUARTS (1.8 L)

Mostarda is a traditional spicy candied fruit condiment from Italy. As such, it goes great with grilled meat and fatty or salty foods. This is a basic recipe—you can substitute other fruits, such as melon (skin on) or all types of citrus or stone fruit.

2 oranges

1 large grapefruit

2 apples

12 cups (2.7 kg) sugar

12 cups (2.8 ml) water

1 cup (240 g) yellow mustard seeds

2 cups (473 ml) mustard seed oil

Use a cake tester to poke 20 holes in the orange and the grapefruit. Use three small pots, each with 4 cups (960 g) sugar and 4 cups (0.95 l) water. Put one piece of fruit in each pot.

Bring to simmer from cold, then to boil. As soon as the water boils, remove the fruit and cool it in the refrigerator. Cool the simple syrup to room temperature. Repeat this process 3 times. Save the liquid all three times. After the third cook, cool the syrup. Peel and chop the fruits and set aside. Add the mustard seeds and oil to the syrup and bring to a boil. Reduce by half, then add the diced fruit and cook on a low simmer for 15 minutes.

Green Tomato Chutney

Yield: 2 quarts (1.8 L)

A lot of farmers come to us with green tomatoes, and you can only pickle or fry so many! I started making chutneys out of them, and this recipe is so popular that we make it in 20-pound batches. The sour, tart flavor of the green tomatoes combined with the sugar yields a sweet-and-sour-flavored chutney that can be served on everything from cheese to Foie Gras Torchon.

4 cloves garlic

1 piece mace

1 broken piece cassia bark

1 lb (450 g) green tomatoes, rough chopped

2 cups (480 g) sugar

¼ cup (60 g) yellow mustard seeds

1 tbsp (15 ml) molasses

2 tbsp (30 ml) white wine vinegar

1 tbsp (15 ml) mustard seed oil

Sachet in cheesecloth: 4 garlic cloves, 1 piece mace and 1 broken piece cassia bark.

Mix the tomatoes with the sugar and let sit overnight in the refrigerator, or at least 12 hours. Combine sugared tomatoes with all other ingredients in a pot. Cook over medium heat for 45 minutes, adding ¼ cup (60 ml) water if it's too thick.

Alternatively, add 1 cup (240 g) chopped Indian lime (right out of the jar) and use over steamed white rice.

Romesco

Romesco is a traditional sauce made in Catalonia, Spain, where it is served during the spring onion festival. This is a delicious sauce that goes well with grilled meats, ham, salami or sausage.

2 dried cascabel chili peppers

1 Spanish onion, julienned

Salt to taste

Pepper to taste

1 cup (237 ml) extra-virgin olive oil

5 cloves of garlic, crushed

1 red bell pepper, chopped and seeds removed

1 red jalapeño pepper, chopped and seeds removed

3 Roma tomatoes, chopped

¾ cup (180 g) marcona (Spanish) almonds, toasted

½ cup (120 g) hazelnuts, toasted

1½ cup (180 ml) water

2 tbsp (30 ml) red wine vinegar

Soak cascabel peppers in water for 1 hour, then remove seeds and chop.

Season onion with salt and pepper, then cook in ½ cup (118 ml) olive oil until tender. Add garlic and cook until tender. Add peppers and cook 5 minutes. Add tomatoes and toasted nuts. Cook for 1 hour, adding ¼ cup (60 ml) water at a time to prevent sticking.

While the mixture is still warm, purée it while adding remaining olive oil and vinegar. Strain if desired. Season with salt and pepper to taste. It keeps, sealed and refrigerated, for 5 days.

Harissa

This is a traditional Arabesque hot sauce that goes well with goat and lamb. In Morocco they add it to many dishes such as couscous. Harissa's unique flavor and texture can bring out the richness of meats, and it goes well with just about anything in this book.

4 dried cascabel chili peppers

1 white onion, chopped

5 cloves of garlic, minced

1 cup (237 ml) olive oil

1 tbsp (15 g) caraway seeds

1 tbsp (15 g) coriander seeds

1 tsp (5 g) yellow mustard seeds

1 tsp (5 g) cumin

1 tbsp (30 g) palm sugar

1 large raw beet, peeled and chopped rough

1 carrot, peeled and chopped rough

Pepper to taste

5 Roma tomatoes, chopped rough

1 cup (237 ml) water

Salt to taste

1 tbsp (30 ml) red wine vinegar

Soak cascabel peppers in water for 1 hour, then remove seeds and chop. Cook onion and garlic in olive oil. When the onion is tender, add caraway, coriander, mustard seeds, cumin, palm sugar, beet, carrot, pepper, tomatoes and cascabel pepper. Cook for 90 minutes over low to medium heat, adding ¼ cup (60 ml) water at a time to prevent sticking. Purée until smooth and season with salt and vinegar. It keeps, sealed and refrigerated, for 5 days.

Green Papaya Relish

Yield: 1 quart (945 ml)

In Thailand they serve a green papaya salad that's really great. I bought some and put it on top of grilled sausage and fell in love. I turned the salad into relish, and I use it on top of Green Curry Sausage (page 18) wrapped in Swiss chard for a Thai version of a hot dog with relish.

2 green papaya

3 cloves of garlic, minced

1 tsp (5 g) ginger

1 red Thai chili, seeds removed

⅓ cup (85 g) palm sugar

¼ cup (60 ml) water

⅓ cup (85 ml) fish sauce

2 tbsp (28 g) cilantro, picked (keep stems)

⅓ cup (85 ml) lime juice

2 tbsp (30 g) chopped mint leaves

Peel the papaya, then grate it with a box grater. Using a food processor or a mortar and pestle, smash the garlic, ginger, red Thai chili, sugar, water, fish sauce, cilantro and stems. The end result should resemble pesto.

Pour this mixture over the papaya, add the lime juice and mint. Stir to combine, cover, and let it sit at room temperature for 6 hours. This will last up to 1 week in the refrigerator.

Tsukemono Pickled Cukes

Yield: 2 quarts (1.8 L)

I love the lightly pickled cucumbers you find on the table in Japanese restaurants. When compared to American pickles, they're more mildly flavored. I like America pickles, but sometimes the acidity can overwhelm certain more subtle flavors of charcuterie. This is a lightly pickled flavor that works well with a variety of grilled sausages and meats, ham or pâté.

2 English cucumbers

2 tbsp (30 g) kosher salt

2 tbsp (30 ml) rice wine vinegar

2 tbsp (30 g) palm sugar

2 tbsp (30 ml) water

1 tbsp (15 g) kombu, soaked and julienned

Wash and dry the cucumbers, then cut them into ½-inch (1.2-cm) thick slices. Put in a bowl and rub all over with kosher salt. Pull the cucumbers out and brush off any remaining salt.

Toss the salted cucumber slices in a bowl with the vinegar, sugar and water. Add the kombu and mix to combine. Pack into jars. Cover the top with plastic wrap, then screw on the lid tightly. Let them sit 12 hours before serving.

Cauliflower Kimchi

Yield: 1 gallon (3.7 L)

If you want to learn about fermenting meats, I recommend learning how to make kimchi, or fermented vegetables, first. This is good training because it shows patience! You can substitute any number of vegetables in this traditional Korean recipe, including cabbage, rutabaga, carrots, radishes or cucumbers.

1 head cauliflower

2 tbsp (30 g) ginger

6 cloves of garlic, minced

1 cup (280 g) coarse Chilean chili flakes

3 red radishes, sliced

1 carrot, peeled and grated

3 sprigs scallion, chopped rough

2 cups (473 ml) fish sauce

¼ cup (60 g) palm sugar

Juice of 2 limes

1 cup (237 ml) water

Chop the head of cauliflower to resemble large pieces of couscous. Combine all ingredients and mix thoroughly. Add 1 cup (237 ml) water, or enough water so that mixture is ¾ covered with water. Put in an airtight container and let it sit in a cool, dry place for 1 week. Check it every day and shake it up if any fuzz appears on the surface. After 1 week it's ready to eat—and it will keep in the refrigerator for up to 30 days.

If you're not patient enough to wait a week, double the amount of lime juice and let the kimchi sit overnight in the refrigerator. It will be ready to eat immediately.

Lentils with Scraps

Yield: 2 quarts (1.8 L)

I love lentils and lentil soup. At the restaurant we often serve things on top of lentils. Around the kitchen there's always some kind of leftover meat around, cooked and uncooked—scraps of sausage on the casing machine, or the end of a salami roll that can't be sliced. I will freeze those pieces, then use them when making lentils for added flavor.

1 cup (240 g) leftover scrap meat

1 white onion, chopped

3 cloves of garlic, minced

1 fresh bay leaf

1 carrot, peeled and chopped

1 rib celery, chopped

Seasoning of choice (e.g., Old Bay, curry, etc.)

2 cups (480 g) lentils

2 cups (473 ml) stock, any kind

Render the scraps with the onion, garlic and bay leaf. Add the carrot and celery and cook 5 minutes. Add the lentils and seasoning of choice.

Heat the stock to a boil. Add the hot stock to the lentils. Cover, then cook in a 300°F (149°C) oven for 20 minutes. This keeps, sealed and refrigerated, for 5 days.

Salsa Verde

Yield: 1 pint (475 ml)

When I was growing up, I was often served mint jelly with boiled meat, and it was the only way to make these bland meats taste good. In some ways salsa verde serves the same purpose, though the meats found in this book bring plenty of rich flavors to the table! Salsa verde works especially well with lean meats, such as tongue and heart. I also like it on top of steamed fish or scrambled eggs. It's salty, sour and fresh.

3 tbsp (45 g) each: mint, tarragon, parsley, sliced chives and scallions

1 shallot, finely diced

1 clove of garlic, minced

1 tbsp (15 ml) fish sauce

2 cups (473 ml) extra-virgin olive oil

¼ cup (60 ml) sherry vinegar

Pinch of espelette chili flakes

Pinch of coarse sea salt, such as fleur de sel

Prepare a chiffonade of the fresh herbs, chives and scallions. Mix with all ingredients and serve. It can keep, sealed and refrigerated, for 5 days.

Paella Rice

55Feeds 6 to 8 people

I love rice, and I make it almost every day, either to eat myself or for someone at the restaurant. Rice is great because it picks up the flavor of whatever you cook it with—so in this recipe the chorizo gives it a rich, full flavor. You can substitute any meat scraps here for variety.

1 cup (240 g) chorizo sausage

1 white onion, julienned

3 cloves of garlic, minced

White portion of 2 scallions, chopped

1 red bell pepper, finely diced

¼ cup (60 m) olive oil

4½ cups (1 l) stock, any type

1 cup (240 g) calasparra (short-grain) rice, aka bomba rice

Pinch of saffron

2 tsp (10 g) kosher salt

Extra-virgin olive oil for garnish

Green portion of 2 scallions, chopped and set aside for garnish

Use a paella pan or a large, very heavy-bottomed pan that is wide enough to fit the rice in a single layer. Cook the chorizo, onion, garlic, scallion whites and red pepper in olive oil until tender.

Bring the stock to a boil in a separate pot.

Add the rice to the paella pan, then stir to coat the rice in fat. Add the saffron and kosher salt and stir to combine.

Add the boiling stock to the paella pan. Cook on high heat until it boils, then turn it down and simmer for 20 minutes. Rotate the pot over the burner if the rice sticks but do not stir. When you hear the rice starting to fry, turn off the heat. Let the rice rest 5 minutes, then scrape it out with a wooden spoon. Drizzle with extra-virgin olive oil and chopped green portion of scallions. This can keep, sealed and refrigerated, for 5 days.

Nuoc Cham

Yield: 3 cups (700 ml)

This is a traditional dipping sauce from the southern part of Vietnam. It's a perfect vinaigrette: salty, sweet, tangy and spicy flavors, all together.

¾ cup (178 ml) warm water

6 oz (170 g) palm sugar

1 cup (237 ml) lime juice

1 cup (237 ml) fish sauce

¼ cup (60 g) minced garlic

¼ cup (60 g) minced ginger

1 cup (240 g) finely shredded carrot

1 tsp (5 g) minced red Thai bird chili, seeds left in

Stir sugar into water to dissolve. Add all other ingredients and stir to combine. Reserve in the refrigerator until ready to use.

Variation

Combine equal parts nuoc cham with cooked liquid from bones (see recipe for Vietnamese Fried Bones, page 118). Called nuoc mam pha, this is a great seasoning for adding to cooked rice and so on.

DASHI

YIELD: 2 GALLONS (7.5 L)

This may seem like a very simple recipe, but because the ingredients can take up to a year to make, the result is a very rich and flavorful broth. Kombu is cured and dried for months, while bonito involves simmering fresh fish, removing the bones, smoking and dehydrating the fish fillets 10 times, then curing for 2-plus weeks. Once the fish is cured until it resembles petrified wood; it is shaved into flakes, a process that takes several weeks to months. This broth makes a great base for many Japanese dishes, including dashi tofu and traditional miso soup. It can keep in a glass container for up to 5 days.

8 oz (227 g) kombu (seaweed)

2 gal (7.5 l) water

8 oz (227 g) bonito (dried/shaved fish)

Soak kombu in cold water for 2 hours. Bring to simmer. As soon as the mixture is simmering, remove the kombu. Spread the bonito evenly over the liquid and bring to boil, then reduce to simmer. As soon as it's simmering, cover it tightly and let it steep for 25 minutes.

When it's done, gently strain it through a fine-mesh sieve. Save the liquid but discard the bonito. Cool dashi in the refrigerator until ready for use.

Schmaltz

Yield: 2 cups (475 ml)

When stored in the refrigerator, schmaltz will keep for weeks. The strained fat and skin can be used to make chicken skin bacon (recipe follows).

1 lb (450 g) chicken fat and skin

1 white onion, diced

Salt

Pepper

Rinse and pound the skin, then chop rough into 1-inch (2.5-cm) pieces. Pat dry, then place in a nonstick pan over low heat. Cover and cook for 15 minutes, stirring occasionally. Turn up heat to medium low and break apart skin. Add white onion and season with salt and pepper. Keep stirring until the fat turns golden brown.

Strain through a fine-mesh sieve. The resulting liquid is schmaltz, a yellowish fat.

The strained skin and fat can be used to make chicken skin bacon. Place the cooked skin and one diced onion in a nonstick pan. Season with salt and pepper and cook on medium heat until golden brown. When the skin is caramelized, dump it onto a tray lined with paper towels. These make a great addition to salad, and they can be made with goose, chicken, turkey or duck skin.

ACKNOWLEDGMENTS

I'd like to thank Will Kiester, Barbara Call, Ken Goodman, Ken Oringer, Jim Bissonnette and Andrew Zimmern.

About
Jamie Bissonnette

Even as a child, Jamie Bissonnette was drawn to the kitchen, eschewing cartoons for cooking shows on the Discovery Channel. With this early start, he earned his Culinary Arts degree from The Art Institute of Fort Lauderdale by the age of 19 and spent his early 20s eating and cooking his way through Paris, San Francisco, New York and Phoenix. These early experiences fed his culinary drive, teaching him expression through his daily-changing menus.

After cooking in Europe and across the United States, Bissonnette settled in Boston and began working in some of the city's most notable kitchens. Following stints at a few highly regarded restaurants, Bissonnette opened Eastern Standard as Executive Chef in 2005. Two years later, he was recruited for the steakhouse KO Prime, winning praise for his modern take on this classic fare. That year in 2007, *The Improper Bostonian* named him "Rising Star Chef" and KO Prime "Best New Restaurant." Shortly after, in the fall of 2008, Bissonnette joined Ken Oringer as Executive Chef and partner of the acclaimed tapas restaurant Toro in Boston's South End, and then together in late 2009 they opened the innovative Italian enoteca Coppa. StarChefs awarded Bissonnette Rising Star Chef that same year. Coppa was then awarded three stars in a rave review from *The Boston Globe* and honorable mention in *Esquire's* "Best New Restaurants" annual list.

Bissonnette is a local champion of nose-to-tail cuisine and is well known locally and nationally for his exceptional charcuterie and passionate dedication to supporting local, sustainable purveyors. He was spokesperson for the Wisconsin Cheese Board in 2008 and has been featured in *The Boston Globe*, *The Wall Street Journal*, *Bon Appétit* and *Edible Boston*, among many other publications.

(continued)

In 2011 he was awarded the prestigious honor of *Food & Wine* magazine's first-ever People's Choice: Best New Chef and he won the $10,000 grand prize on Food Network's *Chopped* series. Bissonnette has also won the James Beard Foundation Award for Best Chef: Northeast.

As chef and owner of Coppa and Toro in Boston, Bissonnette continues to helm the kitchens of both award-winning restaurants and can be found at either (and often both) nightly, overseeing his menus of innovative small plates and nose-to-tail cooking. In 2013 he opened Toro in New York City with partner Ken Oringer.

INDEX

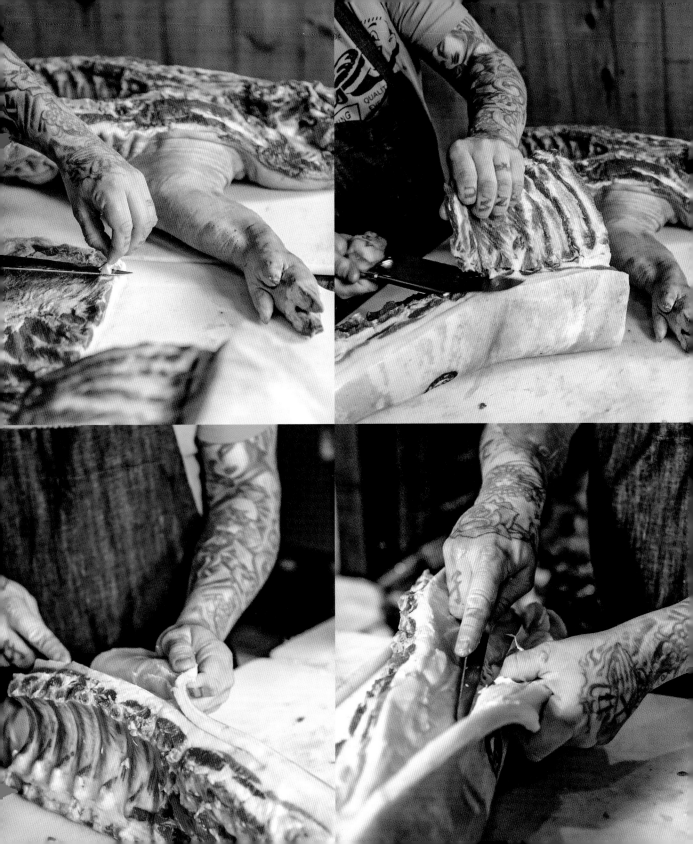

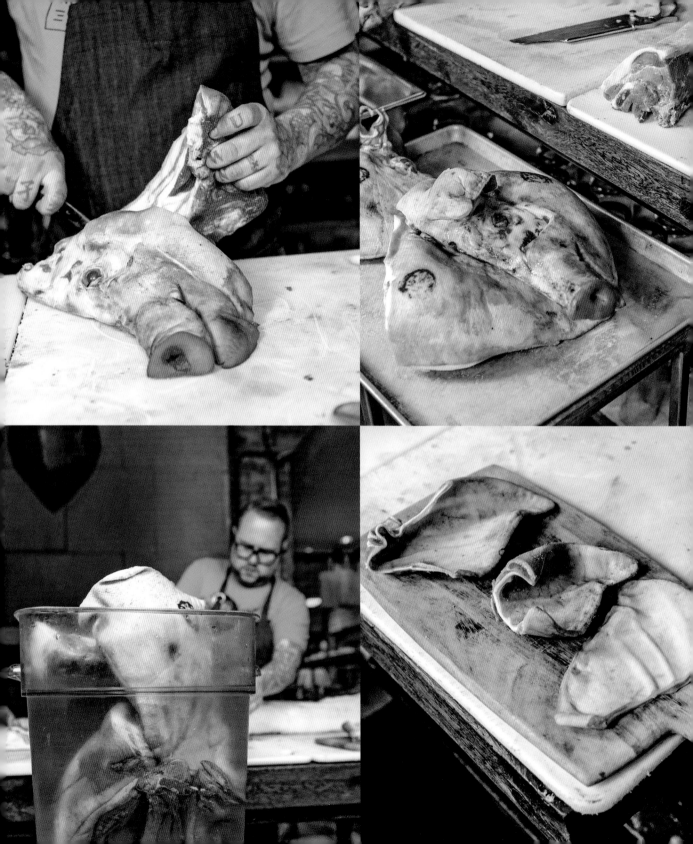